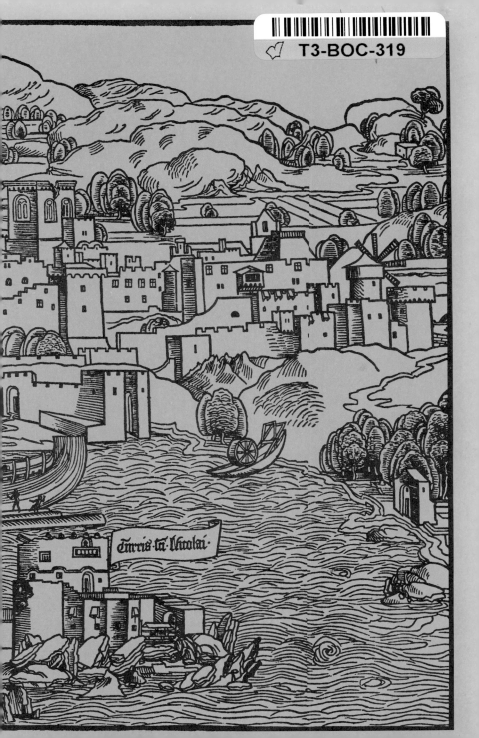

Turris ſā Nicolai·

Lyrics of the Middle Ages

LYRICS
OF
THE
MIDDLE AGES

Edited by HUBERT CREEKMORE

GROVE PRESS, INC. NEW YORK

Grove Press Books and Evergreen Books
are published by Barney Rosset at Grove Press, Inc.
64 University Place   New York 3, N. Y.

Copyright Notices and Acknowledgements

v

Barbara Howes—for her translations of "Rondeau: The Well" and "Ballade: The Hostelry of Thought" by Charles d'Orléans.

The Honourable Society of Cymmrodorion, London—for "The Seagull", "To the Nun", "A Snowy Day" and "He Desires Her Husband's Death" from *Fifty Poems* by Dafydd ap Gwilym, translated by H. Idris Bell and David Bell. Copyright 1942.

Houghton Mifflin Company, Boston—for "Chanson" by Thibaut of Champagne, from *Mont St. Michel and Chartres* by Henry Adams.

Hudson Review—for translations of poems by Guillem IX, Marcabrun and the Monk of Montaudon published in their issue for Summer, 1956.

L. R. Lind—for his translation of "Desperate" by Cino da Pistoia from his anthology *Lyric Poetry of the Italian Renaissance*. Copyright 1954 by the Yale University Press.

Jack Lindsay—for "The Search For Truth", "A Song of Cash", "To Queen Radigunde With Herbs and Violets", "To a Runaway Pupil" and "Good Friday" from his book *Medieval Latin Poets*. Copyright 1934.

Owen Masters—for his translations of six short poems and "Crazy Sweeney's Song of the Woods" in the Irish section.

Harold Matson Company, New York—for "May" from *The Fountain of Magic* by Frank O'Connor. Copyright 1939 by Frank O'Connor. Reprinted by permission of Harold Matson Company.

New Directions, New York—for "The Seafarer" and Cavalcanti's Sonnet "Who is she . . ." from *Translations of Ezra Pound*, copyright 1953; for "Rumor Laetalis" from *The Phoenix and the Tortoise* by Kenneth Rexroth, copyright 1944; for "Ballade of the Hanged Men" from *In the Rose of Time* by Robert Fitzgerald, copyright 1956; for "Tantalos", "Praise of Women" and "Inscription For a Smyrna Privy" from *Poems From the Greek Anthology* by Dudley Fitts, copyright 1956; for "Dum Diana Vitrea", "Flowering Time" and "Confession of Golias" from *The Goliard Poets* by George Whicher, copyright 1949.

O. L. Oliver—for his translations of "Death Song of Haakon the Good" by Eyvindr Finsson, "Dawn Song" by Dietmar von Aist and "Under the Linden" by Walther von der Vogelweide.

Contents

ix

xi

Introduction

The literature of the Middle Ages has been unduly neglected in this century, especially in the lyric phase, by both the teacher and the reader. For the reader, let it be said that he has had scant opportunity to do otherwise than neglect, unless he sought out old books in a library. New books have offered him little more than the scattered introductory sections in anthologies of translation, and the scholarly collections of early English poetry. Two or three recent anthologies of medieval writing give so little lyric poetry that it seems to have been considered rather a necessary blemish among the pages of prose than a brilliant manifestation of the spirit of the times. This collection is intended to fill the gap in a modest way, but is not a remedy for academic deficiencies I may touch upon later. It is, I believe, the first anthology to present only medieval poetry in translation in a broader than national scope.

As for those teachers whom I charged at the outset, they tend, in the main, to stress medieval historical events, social and economic revolutions, and religious thought. When they turn to literature at all, it is usually to the long narrative poems, romances and epics. The student has, it is true, in English courses, a smattering of medieval creative writing before Chaucer tossed at him—*The Shepherd's Play* or *Everyman*, fragments from *Morte Arthur* or *Gawaine and the Green Knight*, *Beowulf*, and a handful of lyrics. The effect of this isolation from the main stream of European literature, in lyric poetry particularly, is to instill in the student* the notion that for a

---

* In "student" I refer to the candidate for the baccalaureate, who has certain required literary courses to complete, not to the student in specialized fields.

thousand years almost nothing was written that might interest him. It is, then, easy for him to accept the term, "Dark Ages", and seek brighter reading matter elsewhere.

To remedy this deficiency poses a problem of curriculum, admittedly, but not to do so leaves a need in the graduate's understanding and appreciation of even our own English poetry, unless the teacher, on his own initiative, is willing and able to fill it. Many, I am sure, try to do so; many others very likely do not or can not. Students of the latter may gain the knowledge that, for example, Wyatt and Surrey wrote the first sonnets in English, a fact most of them remember at least until the award of their diplomas, but where do they think those sonnets came from? Or do they ever wonder?

If this seems to be carping over a minor point, let me say that it is indicative of the weakness, if not the failure, of our whole educational system below the graduate level. If our conduct of mass public education over these many decades were successful, we should surely be a much different country than we are. As it is, numbers of people have forfeited good peasant common sense to a mere college degree and thereafter ceased using their senses. There are signs that we shall soon wake up, at least in the scientific field. But as to literature—and some of it provides very special fission bombs that governments, even industries, wish to abolish or control. . . .

In our contemporary Dark Age, with education reduced to such a fiasco that the majority of our citizens cannot cope with the feeble challenge of television's banalities, to say nothing of individual thought, even the college man might pigeonhole Western writing into a classical group of Greek and Roman works, a Renaissance group of English works, and some later "Ages" and "Schools" of English writing. That is to say, he knows a bit of the beginning (500 B.C. to A.D. 500) and something of the ending (1500 to the present), but he is only dimly aware that there was a second millenium between the other two. Though he is forced to discover something of literatures other than English in Humanities classes, he gets little of the continuity of literature in its formative phases for many of the

"Ages" he must study. The entire middle period, the bridge from classical to modern literature over which themes, techniques, attitudes, forms and emotions flowed and were transformed into the modern temperament, is ignored or barely mentioned, with a consequent ignorance of and inability to deal with the intent of much serious modern writing.

As noted above, the historic, social, economic and religious developments of this age of evolution and revolution are usually touched upon in one college course or another which the student will attend. But the European evolution of language and literature, the essential background of many English courses he will have to take, is usually glossed over. For such studies, since a large part of the material under discussion will be lyric poetry, the European medieval lyric is more pertinent—as it is to present-day life and enjoyment—than familiarity with the Children's Crusade, feudalism, the Battle of Tours, the Hanseatic League, the Black Death, simony, schisms and the sale of indulgences. I do not mean that it is not good to know those things and many more; fertile minds can make use of the knowledge. But unfortunately for us contemporary people, the more we learn of history, the fewer lessons we learn from it. What we learn from poetry, if it is good, is always with us and always valid.

The Middle Ages, then, are the time when the modern European languages evolved from earlier tongues—Irish and Welsh from the old forms; Scandinavian, German, Dutch and English from the Germanic group of languages; and Provençal, French, Spanish, Portuguese and Italian from the Latin. They are the time when modern poetry was born and developed, beginning a long line of progeny that continues to the present. If they are sometimes called "Dark", it should be recalled that among other things, they are the ages of the marvels of Gothic architecture and painting, of the development of modern music on a polyphonic scale and of great human spirits in all fields of activity. Compared with the glow of the succeeding Renaissance, their offspring, they seem dark. And, like our own century, they were indeed a period of confusion and upheaval in politics, of cynical corruption (especially in religion), of barbarian invasions, of extremes of wealth and poverty, of persecutions and fears and flagrant wrong-doing. To that darkness can be added the shadow of plagues and sudden early death—but not of anti-intelligence and atomic clouds. Despite the forbidding air of this era in such a capsule characterization, it produced quantities of beautiful enduring work in every artistic medium. In poetry it reached its climax in a group of the world's greatest poets: Chaucer in England, Dafydd ap Gwilym in Wales, Villon in France, Petrarch and Dante in Italy.

Except for Dafydd ap Gwilym, whose work suffers the relative isolation of a severe language barrier, these poets are familiar in varying degrees to the majority of serious readers and periodically have had some influence on poets after them. They or their works continue to be used for other poems, for novels, plays, operas, musical shows. There are even recent translations of much of their poetry, and interest in Dante surged to new heights only a decade or so ago, spurred by T. S. Eliot, Ezra Pound and the literary critics who followed them.

But ours is probably not a century that will take enthusiastically to the tranquil and meditative allure of most medieval writing. We, especially in the United States, like more shocks and gore, more action and frenzy, in our creative writing, and less delicacy, less contemplation, technique, beauty or reasoning than the Middle Ages can give us. Yet much of our poetry today suffers from ignorance equally of medieval poetry and of the Greek and Roman poetry that preceded it. (The study of the classic languages faded from most colleges after the 1920's.) We have, of course, our own brand-new inventions and approaches to poetry. But if one should wonder at the power of such a man as Ezra Pound in poetic invention and technique, as compared with hosts of imitators and antagonists, it should be remembered that he learned and never forsook the classic and medieval authors. To "make it new", in his Chinese motto, one must know just what one is to make new, and how.

Others in this century than Ezra Pound have, of course, turned to medieval materials for literary form and subject.

Aside from the ever-present "historical" novel of many a sort and degree, one thinks primarily of Edna St. Vincent Millay's *The King's Henchman* (1928) and the trilogy by Edwin Arlington Robinson—*Merlin* (1917), *Lancelot* (1920) and *Tristram* (1927). These books use the most popular themes of medieval romance —Arthurian legend and Tristram and Isolde—just as many of the nineteenth-century poets did. In more recent years, W. H. Auden has revived the sestina form and used the Anglo-Saxon alliterative line, though his material remains contemporary.

The nineteenth century, however, took the Middle Ages to its heart more warmly than any since the Renaissance. In the 90's, William Morris was issuing from his Kelmscott Press elaborate editions of Arthurian tales and was writing and translating in the medieval field. Somewhat earlier, Andrew Lang had translated *Aucassin and Nicolete*, which surely must have been a rival of FitzGerald's *Rubaiyat* as a lover's gift book, though how opposite! Lang had also collected many medieval fairy tales and lyric poems. Tennyson had written the *Idylls of the King*, and the Pre-Raphaelite Brotherhood was publishing medieval Italian poets, translated mainly by Rossetti, in their journal, *The Germ*. Medieval subjects were favorites of Robert Browning. Many English poets, and French, as well, revived the rondeau and adopted the ballade as a favorite form: Scott, Southey, Swinburne, Rossetti, Lang, Henley, Dobson and Chesterton, to name a few. Perhaps the reason for all this popularity of the Middle Ages was that a great deal of the important research and dissemination of new knowledge about the period was then being done.

I do not recommend that we return to such concentrated immersion in medieval literature. There are, after all, a few more challenging matters in the world today that need most of our attention. But while we struggle with the ugly life we have been busily creating, let us not completely overlook all the riches and beauty that our predecessors have left us. They can be very useful at times.

It has already been suggested that this is the first anthology of its kind. To the best of my knowledge, this is true*. The contents, restricted to lyric poetry of the Middle Ages (which for my purposes are considered to be those between 500 and 1500), are drawn from translations of poetry in fourteen major European languages. Each section has a short preface dealing more specifically with the language, the poetry and the forms. Oriental literatures have been excluded because of their slight relation to the European lyrics (despite arguments for Arabian influence on some of the literatures), and because of limitations of space.

The poems are presented in four roughly defined groups: Classical, Romance, Gaelic and Germanic. Though literature was being produced in other European countries and languages before the end of the Middle Ages—notably in Czech, Polish and Russian—little of it is lyric, and that not particularly inviting in the translations available. Their major poetic works were written after 1500.

The basis of selection has been, first, availability and quality of translation, considering, of course, that the original seemed worth the effort of translating; and second, avoidance of too much duplication of forms unless fresh themes or treatments appear. Wherever possible, I have given the complete poem, but it should be understood that some of these are actually parts of longer sequences of separate poems—e.g., the selections from Aneirin, the *Elder Edda*, Boethius, Marie de France, Villon. Because of avoiding abridgments for the most part, and narrative poetry altogether, this book unfortunately cannot present the best of Chaucer or Dante. As exceptions to the rule against abridgments, two poems, so treated because of digressions, repetitions or diffuseness, may be cited: "Crazy Sweeny's Song of the Woods" and "The Beginning and the End".

* A similar collection, with a long helpful introduction, is *The Medieval Latin and Romance Lyric to A.D. 1300* by Fred Brittain (Cambridge, 1937). It contains poems in six languages (Latin and its five derivatives) but none are translated. There are numerous books of translated medieval poetry, from which some of the poems herein were chosen, but each is limited to a single language or language group.

Many poems appear here in hitherto unpublished translations and some, notably the entire Portuguese group, are translated into English for the first time.

It is hoped that this collection, brief though it is, will serve to show the rich resources for present-day stimulation and entertainment, as well as the old-time lustiness, gaiety, affection, sorrow, laughter, wonder and piety, of an era too often considered drab.

New York City, 1958   HUBERT CREEKMORE

Greek

*T*he spirit and energy of the great classical literature of Greece, *beginning with the* Iliad *and the* Odyssey, *were changing, if not fading, by the time of the Alexandrian period in the third century* B.C. *The splendor, nobility and vision of the early epics and dramas were slowly giving way to learned, nostalgic, and hence inevitably imitative work, though not without charm in its intimacy of psychological revelation and its technical achievement. The epigram, as seen in the Greek Anthology, with its elegiac mood, its scholarly reference, or its bitter sophistication, seems the most comfortable literary form for the temper of these Hellenistic poets.*

This form continued in favor until the Byzantine period, which began after the fall of the Western Roman Empire in 476 A.D., *but when that event ushered in the Middle Ages, almost no poetry of consequence was being written in Greek. The three poets given here are perhaps the best representatives of this waning era of poetry, and in these translations come through as quite lively and contemporary. But aside from the few lyrics, epigrams, epics and pseudo-epics, the rest of*

3

literature was prose: history, theology, philosophy, sermons, commentaries, exegeses, doctrinal tracts—a vigorous torrent of words to have so little vitality today. The decline of classic Greek literature had entered its last phase.

A final blow to the poetic spirit came with Justinian's closing, in 529, of the schools of heathen philosophy because they were too "symbolic". With this prohibition, much of the ferment and body of concepts that might tend to the creation of poetry were cut away from later writers. Pagan ideas yielded to Christian ideas, and by the seventh century had almost entirely vanished. Thereafter, Greek poetry was influenced not only by Christianity but by the literary forms and social conventions of newer European literatures.

PALLADAS (*fl.* 400)

Praise of Women

Only twice is womankind
Anything but an affliction:

(1) in bride-bed
&
(2) in the grave.

[DUDLEY FITTS]

O Man, Remember

O man, remember how your father got you—
remember well and void your vanity.
Plato's dreams have stuffed you full of pride,
with talk that you're immortal and divine.
But you are formed of dust, no cause for boasting,
and even then the notion's prettified.
To call a spade a spade, you were born
of wanton lust and a filthy drop of sperm.

[D. L. FELDSTONE]

PAULUS SILENTIARIUS (d. 575)

Tantalos

Mouth to mouth joined we lie, her naked breasts
Curved to my fingers, my fury grazing deep
On the silver plain of her throat,
                            and then: no more.
She denies me her bed. Half of her body to Love
She has given, half to Prudence:
                            I die between.

[DUDLEY FITTS]

AGATHIAS SCHOLASTICUS (*c.* 536–*c.* 582)

Inscription For a Smyrna Privy

And so your head aches, friend? and so
Your heavy body groans with sluggishness,
And you must knead your paunch with both hands to dislodge
The delicious work of your jaws?

What a fool!

Then was the time to think of it when you lay,
Most hog-like, gorging at table, in love with your own
Capacity.   And so, well may you sit here now:
The latter end of all your delight is this,
That you pummel your belly for the sins your throat committed.

[DUDLEY FITTS]

Latin

Taking its impetus, by translation and imitation, from Alexandrian Greek works, Latin progressed to the molding of a creative literature of its own. Great writers produced elegy, lyric, epic, didactic, satiric and philosophical poetry for about 250 years, but after the time of Juvenal (d. 140) the sturdy inventive spirit seemed to flag. The correlation of this waning with the decay of the national spirit may be important. For the Roman Empire began its slow decline with the death of Marcus Aurelius (180 A.D.) and went on crumbling through later dissolute emperors and invasions of Vandals and Visigoths to its final collapse in 476.

During this long period, the Christian faith had been spreading, and after the fall of the empire it rapidly overcame most of the pagan religions. Until the mid-thirteenth century, the church had used Greek; then it switched to Latin, and Latin found salvation. Because of that, long afterward it was able "to pass itself off as a living language when it had been dead for centuries", and even today survives in the Roman Church. The language, however, was quite alive in these early centuries throughout Romanized Europe, though in various dialects.

7

Writers clung to the devitalized traditional usage, but even this was weakened when at the end of the fourth century St. Jerome completed the Vulgate Bible, *rendered in the natural vulgar Latin of the day. In* 813 *the Council of Tours ordered the clergy to preach in the Romanic vernacular and soon the breach between classic Latin and its Romance progeny was swiftly widening. Thus, the Church, while retaining Latin as its own speech, had much to do with abolishing it as popular speech.*

Along with the Church, the universities and the legal profession held to the older, now degraded, language. Authors too, most of whom were indeed clerics, scholars or lawyers, continued to write in Latin. But the Low Latin speech, lingua romana, *was breaking up and changing, and so were the laws of its prosody. The quantitative metric principle of classic poets slowly broke down; the feeling and necessity for it were lost and consequently it became unusable. A new technique of form through rhyme and accentual meter was coming in, right along with the rise of vernacular lyrics using the same methods. But this new verse was not too common until the twelfth century.*

Claudius Claudianus, the last pagan poet, wrote in classical meters. So did most of the poets before the era of the Goliards—the wandering scholars, such as the Archpoet of Cologne, and the anonymous singers of the lyrics, sensuous, satiric, humorous, and bibulous.

In some degree, Abelard belongs with them, for he wrote many an impassioned poem to his Heloise, though all are lost to us except those which may be "attributed". Still, it seems unlikely that these love poems, which were so popular in their day that students all over France sang them in the streets and taverns, should have completely vanished. The manuscripts of them, yes—destroyed by Abelard as a penance—but some lusty scholar may have set one or two down from memory, in such songbooks as the Carmina Burana. *Abelard's known poetry consists of a series of Biblical laments and ninety-three hymns for the Breviary of the Paraclete.*

There is, not surprisingly, a vast body of religious verse, written in praise and awe of the Lord during these first centuries of Christian enthusiasm. In translation much of it now seems flat and unoriginal. Of the dozen or so greatest hymns, those by Venantius Fortunatus and Thomas of Celano, and the anonymous Veni Creator Spiritus *are the most noteworthy.*

It is heart-warming but pathetic to see Latin, in the last years before its real extinction, blooming so youthfully with lyrics of a modern temper, just as were the infant languages all about. But by the end of the fourteenth century, the vital poetic essence had departed from the language and found a new haven in its offspring—the Romance tongues of early Provençal, French, Portuguese, Spanish and Italian. During the Renaissance, the language somewhat revived, at least in usage by Humanist poets and philosophers, and an ever thinning stream of writings in Latin has continued to the present day.

CLAUDIUS CLAUDIANUS (d. *c.* 408)

The Old Man of Verona

Happy the man, who his whole time doth bound
Within th' inclosure of his little ground,
Happy the man whom the same humble place,
The hereditary cottage of his race,
From his first rising infancy has known,
And by degrees sees gently bending down,
With natural propension, to that earth
Which both preserved his life, and gave him birth.
Him no false distant lights, by fortune set,
Could ever into foolish wanderings get.
He never dangers either saw or feared:
The dreadful storms at sea he never heard.
He never heard the shrill alarms of war,
Or the worse noises of the lawyers' bar.

No change of consuls marks to him the year;
The change of seasons is his calendar.
The cold and heat, winter and summer shows;
Autumn by fruits, and spring by flowers, he knows.
He measures time by landmarks, and has found
For the whole day the dial of his ground.
A neighboring wood, born with himself, he sees,
And loves his old contemporary trees.
He has only heard of near Verona's name,
And knows it, like the Indies, but by fame.
Does with a like concernment notice take
Of the Red sea, and of Benacus' lake.
Thus health and strength he to a third age enjoys,
And sees a long posterity of boys.
About the spacious world let others roam,
The voyage, life, is longest made at home.

[ABRAHAM COWLEY]

BOETHIUS (c. 480–524)

The Search for Truth

What discord at the heart of things
destroys the pact? What god has set
this war between two truths, until
singly they stand our test and yet
together form a strife of will?

Is truth a single harmony?
Each life to its own purpose clings;
and yet the flesh-entangled soul,
using a smothered fire, can't see
the subtle links that bind the whole.

But why such anxious zeal to tear
the mocking veils and look behind?
Of what we seek, are we aware?
Then why such toil if all is known?
Yet otherwise the search is blind.

What we've not known we cannot need,
an unseen banner cannot lead.
How could we find, or, having found,
how should we know we'd reached the goal?

In contact with the great Alone,
is it the whole or parts we mind?
Though by our cloudy senses bound,
the self has memories that endure;
it drops the parts, yet grasps the whole.

Then he that seeks the truth must fall
on paradox. He'll neither grip
nor yet forget, within, the All;
but still he seeks the Truth he saw,
to handle it and learn its law
by adding truths that he let slip
    to those he kept secure.

[JACK LINDSAY]

VENANTIUS FORTUNATUS (*c.* 530–610?)

Hymn to the Holy Cross

The royal banners forward go;
The cross shines forth in mystic glow,
Where he in flesh, our flesh who made,
Upon the tree of pain is laid.

Behold! the nails, with anguish fierce,
His outstretched hands and vitals pierce!
Here, our redemption to obtain,
The mighty sacrifice is slain!

Where deep for us the spear has dyed,
Life's torrent rushing from his side,
To wash us in that precious flood
Where mingled water flowed and blood.

Fulfilled is all that David told
In true prophetic song of old;
Amidst the nations, God (saith he)
Hath reigned and triumphed from the Tree.

O Tree of beauty! Tree of light!
O Tree with royal purple dight!
Elect on whose triumphal breast
Those holy limbs should find their rest!

On whose dear arms, so widely flung,
The weight of this world's ransom hung:
The price of human kind to pay,
And spoil the spoiler of his prey.

With fragrance dropping from each bough,
Sweeter than sweetest nectar thou,
Decked with the fruit of peace and praise,
And glorious with triumphal lays.

Hail, Altar! Hail, O Victim, thee
Decks now thy passion's victory;
Where life for sinners death endured,
And life by death for man procured.

[J. M. NEALE, *revised by Chambers*]

To Queen Radigunde with Herbs and Violets

If lilies now had come to candid birth
or roses, soft with crimson, met the eye,
grown wild or plucked from my small plot of earth,
I'd send them, lowly things, to one so high.
But lacking these, with humbler herbs I'll try.
Love makes a vetch a rose; and as you'll see
amid these fragrant herbs of mine there lie
the purple violets for nobility.
For they both breathe a royal murex-dye
and tinge with grace and scent the greenery:
two qualities that we may know you by.
Their beauty is a scent eternally.

[JACK LINDSAY]

ALCUIN (735–804)

To a Run-away Pupil

O cuckoo, once your song was loud and gay,
what fate has raped away your melodies?
O cuckoo, cuckoo, cursèd was the day
that lured your music from our sheltering trees.
All men bewail the cuckoo's wandering.
"The cuckoo's gone, alas, my cuckoo's dead."
No, he's not dead. He'll come another spring
and bring us back the merriment that's fled.

Who knows the day? I fear the waves, and weep:
The whirlpool sucks, the billows choke his breath.
Woe if the wine-god whelmed him in the deep
that gapes for youth with water-jaws of death.
Yet, if he lives, he'll find the nests of home,
returning safe from fiercely pecking crows.
O cuckoo, who seduced your heart to roam?
You're gone, you're gone, and where you are, none knows.

If songs you love, then, cuckoo, hurry back.
Come back, I beg you, stretch your wings and skim.
O cuckoo, flutter down the homeward track.
Young Daphnis sighs for you, his eyes are dim.
The spring is here. O cuckoo, break your sleep.
Father Menalcar sighs, he holds you dear.
The oxen browse, the meadowgrass is deep,
but where's the cuckoo? Only he's not here.

O wail the cuckoo, wail him everywhere.
Merry, he went. Returning, will he moan?
If he'll but come, then with his tears we'll bear,
we'll wail with him, he shall not weep alone.

O wail your fate, my lad so well endowed,
and let your bowels quake to hear the wail.
Unless a flint begot you, wail aloud;
think of the past, and tears can hardly fail.
For if a father lost the boy he's bred,
would he not weep to ease his heart of pain?
And if a brother saw a brother dead,
what would he do but weep and weep again?

Three lives, with but a single heart, were we:
now scarcely two, because the third is fled,
fled from us, fled. There's only misery:
the cuckoo's gone, and we have tears to shed.
Send him a song, a song of our distress;
for songs will bring him back, if tales are true.
Yet, anywhere, I wish him happiness.
Remember us, that's all. Good luck to you.

[JACK LINDSAY]

WALAFRID STRABO (809–849)

To His Friend in Absence

When the moon's splendour shines in naked heaven,
　　Stand thou and gaze beneath the open sky.
See how that radiance from her lamp is riven,
　　And in one splendour foldeth gloriously
Two that have loved, and now divided far,
Bound by love's bond, in heart together are.

What though thy lover's eyes in vain desire thee,
  Seek for love's face, and find that face denied?
Let that light be between us for a token;
  Take this poor verse that love and faith inscribe.
Love, art thou true? and fast love's chain about thee?
Then for all time, O love, God give thee joy!

[HELEN WADDELL]

PETER ABELARD (1079–1142)

Good Friday

Alone, dear Lord, to sacrifice you go,
submitting to the death your coming breaks.
What can we say when wretchedly we know
that you are suffering for our sinful sakes?

We, we have sinned, to us the pain is due:
why must you then be punished for our deed?
O pierce our breasts to suffer here with you,
then our compassion may for mercy plead.

Now in the dark we weep, a three days' space,
a dusk of loss where tears forever start,
until the dawn uplifts her joyous face
and Christ is risen in each sorrowing heart.

Christ, make us bleed with pity for your end,
that in your glory we may find a place.
When three long days in hopeless grief we spend,
you yield the laughter of your paschal grace.

[JACK LINDSAY]

ATTRIBUTED TO ABELARD

Rumor Laetalis

I am constantly wounded
By the deadly gossip that adds
Insult to injury, that
Punished me mercilessly
With the news of your latest
Scandal in my ears. Wherever
I go the smirking fame of each
Fresh despicable infamy
Has run on ahead of me.
Can't you learn to be cautious
About your lecheries?
Hide your practices in darkness;
Keep away from raised eyebrows.
If you must murder love, do it
Covertly, with your candied
Prurience and murmured lewdness.

You were never the heroine
Of dirty stories in the days
When love bound us together.
Now those links are broken, desire
Is frozen, and you are free
To indulge every morbid lust,
And filthy jokes about your
Latest amour are the delight
Of every cocktail party.
Your boudoir is a brothel,
Your salon is a saloon;
Even your sensibilities
And your depraved innocence
Are only special premiums,
Rewards of a shameful commerce.

O the heartbreaking memory
Of days like flowers, and your
Eyes that shone like Venus the star
In our brief nights, and the soft bird
Flight of your love about me;
And now your eyes are as bitter
As a rattlesnake's dead eyes,
And your disdain as malignant.
Those who give off the smell of coin
You warm in bed; I who have
Love to bring am not even
Allowed to speak to you now.
You receive charlatans and fools;
I have only the swindling
Memory of poisoned honey.

[KENNETH REXROTH]

Dum Diana Vitrea

When Diana's gleaming lamp,
Upward gliding, rises late,
Kindled while her brother's light,
Fading, still is roseate,
Sweet airs blowing from the west
Lift the mists that congregate
Far aloft:
Like music soft
Twilight soothes the breast,
And after long repelling
The heart gives love a dwelling.
Welcome then
To mortal men,
Hesperus, shining bright,
Brings cool and damp
The sleep-compelling dews of night.

O what bliss it is!
Sleep, the antidote,
From storms of care and grief
How sheltered, how remote:
Sleep that slyly enters
The portals of the eyes,
Bringing joys that equal
Sweet love's paradise.

When Morpheus has passed
To drowsy fancy sending
A light wind blowing,
Ripe corn bending,
Rippling waters flowing
Over pure sands,
Millwheels turning
While still the mill stands,
Then robbed of all discerning
The eyes close at last.

After the subtle interchange of love
The nerves, late overtaxed,
Are now relaxed;
A wondrous newness we are conscious of,
While eyes afloat
With darkness brimming
Glide like a boat
On eyelids skimming.
Heigh, 'tis joy to disencumber
Thought from coils of love in slumber,
But sweeter far the reawaking
Out of sleep to new love-making.

From glad satiety such fumes arise
As cloud the three-celled brain;
These vapors then incline the heavy eyes
To sleep again,
Filling the eyelids with a drowsy smoke
That holds in check the power of sight;
The animal spirits, ministering, wrap tight
The eyes as with a cloak.

Then under pleasant boughs,
While grieving Philomel descants,
Sweet it is to drowse,
Or still more sweet perchance
To woo some pretty creature on the lawn:
Spicy garden odors breathing,
Roses round our couch enwreathing,
To snatch delight in slumber's sustenance,
Love's fainting joys a while forgone
In languor deep withdrawn.

But O, how many are the changes
Through which a lover's spirit ranges!
No ship that drifts
With anchor lost
Can match the shifts
Of hope and fear
Wherewith he's crossed:
The folk of Venus buy her service dear.

[GEORGE F. WHICHER]

THE ARCHPOET OF COLOGNE (1130?–1165?)

The Confession of Golias

Indignation's fiery flood
   Scalds my inmost being;
I must chew a bitter cud,
   One conclusion seeing:
Light of substance is my blood,
   Restlessness decreeing,
So that down the wind I scud
   Like a dead leaf fleeing.

Let the wise man place his seat
   On the rock firm founded.
Hither, thither, I must beat
   By my follies hounded.
With the flowing stream I fleet,
   So my doom is sounded;
'Neath the arch of heaven my feet
   Nowhere yet have grounded.

Like a hapless ship I fare
   Left without a sailor,
Like a bird on ways of air,
   Some poor lost cloud-scaler;
Not a jot for chains I care,
   Not for key nor jailer.
Sinful flesh is frail, I swear.
   Mine's the same—but frailer!

Dull and dour sobriety
   Never takes my money,
Give me loose society
   Where the jokes are funny;
Love will bring variety,
   Toil that's sweet as honey.
Pillars of propriety,
   Have you hearts as sunny?

Down the primrose path I post
　　Straight to Satan's grotto,
Shunning virtue, doing most
　　Things that I ought not to;
Little hope of heaven I boast,
　　Charmed by pleasure's otto:
Since the soul is bound to roast
　　Save the skin's my motto.

Hear me, prelate most discreet,
　　For indulgence crying:
Deadly sin I found so sweet
　　I'm in love with dying;
Every pretty girl I meet
　　Sets my heart a-sighing:
Hands off! ah, but in conceit
　　In her arms I'm lying.

Much too hard it is, I find,
　　So to change my essence
As to keep a virgin mind
　　In a virgin's presence.
Rigid laws can never bind
　　Youth to acquiescence;
Light o' loves must seek their kind,
　　Bodies take their pleasance.

Who that in a bonfire falls
　　Is not scorched by flame there?
Who can leave Pavia's walls
　　Pure as when he came there?
Venus' beckoning finger calls
　　Youths with sportive aim there,
Eyes make captive willing thralls,
　　Faces hunt for game there.

Give the chaste Hippolytus
    One day in Pavia,
He'll not long be virtuous;
    Next day you will see a
Lover most solicitous.
    Love's their one idea:
'Mid these towers so numerous
    Dwells no Alethea.

Next, I'm called in terms precise
    Monstrous fond of gaming;
Losing all my clothes at dice
    Gains me this worth naming:
While outside I'm cool as ice,
    Inwardly I'm flaming,
Then with daintiest device
    Poems and songs I'm framing.

Third, the tavern—here I dread
    Lies detraction's kernel:
Long on tavern joys I've fed,
    Never shall I spurn all
Till these eyes shall see instead
    Choirs from realms supernal
Chanting for the newly dead
    Requiem eternal.

My intention is to die
    In the tavern drinking;
Wine must be at hand, for I
    Want it when I'm sinking.
Angels when they come shall cry,
    At my frailties winking:
"Spare this drunkard, God, he's high,
    Absolutely stinking!"

Cups of wine illuminate
  Beacons of the spirit,
Draughts of nectar elevate
  Hearts to heaven, or near it.
Give me tavern liquor straight,
  Gouty lords may fear it—
Pah! their watered stuff I hate.
  Drawer, do you hear it?

Public life, there's no mistake,
  Certain poets find irking;
Courts they willingly forsake,
  In seclusion lurking;
There they study, drudge, and wake,
  No endeavor shirking,
Hoping one great poem to make
  Ere they cease from working.

Starveling rhymesters, when they thirst
  Water is their potion!
City din they count accurst
  And the crowd's commotion.
Foundlings by the Muses nursed,
  Fame's their only notion:
Fame they sometimes win, but first
  Die of their devotion.

Nature grants us each a prize,
  Fitly used, it waxes;
Mine in verse—not fasting—lies.
  Fasting so relaxes,
Any stripling half my size
  Bumps me off my axis.
Thirst and fasting I despise
  Worse than death and taxes.

One free gift from nature's stock
   Each man draws, and rightly;
Mine's for verse and getting chock
   Full of liquor nightly.
Broach the landlord's oldest crock
   Till I've mellowed slightly:
Good wine makes the fancies flock
   Copiously and brightly.

Let the verse be as the wine.
   Grasp this true technique well,
And like me, until you dine,
   Neither write nor speak well.
Fasting, while I peak and pine,
   Nothing comes in sequel;
Feast me, and these songs of mine
   Ovid could not equal.

Inspiration's wooed in vain,
   Fancy stays retired,
Till my craving guts obtain
   All they have desired;
Then let mighty Bacchus reign
   Till I'm duly fired,
Phoebus rushes to my brain—
   Lord, but I'm inspired!

Thus I stand condemned, but by
   My own accusation;
See, the courtiers prophesy
   My deserved damnation;
Yet not one can testify,
   For his own salvation,
He is better armed than I
   'Gainst the world's temptation.

Even here before thy throne,
   Prince and true confessor,
Following the rule made known
   By our Intercessor,
Let him cast at me the stone,
   Be the bard's oppressor,
Who can swear that he alone
   Never was transgressor.

See, I've labored to record
   All my heart confesses;
Fulsome brews from pleasure's board—
   I spit out the messes!
Changed at last, I hasten toward
   This new life that blesses.
Man sees but the face; thou, Lord,
   Knowest the heart's recesses.

Now to virtue reconciled
   Base desires I quiet,
Sweep and scour my sin-defiled
   Soul to purify it.
See me now a new-born child,
   New milk is my diet;
In my heart no more shall wild
   Vanities run riot.

Gracious Prince, Cologne's elect,
   Archbishop and warden,
Grant me mercy, nor reject
   One who sues for pardon.
Deign my penance to direct,
   Lest my heart should harden,
No commands will I neglect:
   Plant me in thy garden.

Pity me, thy suppliant,
  Let no thunder rumble.
Lion, king of beasts, doth grant
  Mercy to the humble.
O ye kings, were mercy scant
  Heaven itself would crumble.
Tasting bitters when they want
  Sweets will make men grumble.
                              [GEORGE F. WHICHER]

ANONYMOUS (12th century)

Flora

Rudely blows the winter blast,
Withered leaves are falling fast,
Cold hath hushed the birds at last.
  While the heavens were warm and glowing,
    Nature's offspring loved in May;
  But man's heart no debt is owing
    To such change of month or day
    As the dumb brute-beasts obey.
Oh, the joys of this possessing!
How unspeakable the blessing
  That my Flora yields today!

Labor long I did not rue,
Ere I won my wages due,
And the prize I played for drew.
  Flora with her brows of laughter,
    Gazing on me, breathing bliss,
  Draws my yearning spirit after,
    Sucks my soul forth in a kiss:
    Where's the pastime matched with this?
Oh, the joys of this possessing!
How unspeakable the blessing
  Of my Flora's loveliness!

Truly mine is no harsh doom,
While in this secluded room
Venus lights for me the gloom!
  Flora faultless as a blossom
    Bares her smooth limbs for mine eyes;
  Softly shines her virgin bosom,
    And the breasts that gently rise
    Like the hills of Paradise.
Oh, the joys of this possessing!
How unspeakable the blessing
  When my Flora is the prize!

From her tender breasts decline,
In a gradual curving line,
Flanks like swansdown white and fine.
  On her skin the touch discerneth
    Naught of rough; 'tis soft as snow:
  'Neath the waist her belly turneth
    Unto fulness, where below
    In Love's garden lilies blow.
Oh, the joys of this possessing!
How unspeakable the blessing,
  Sweetest sweets from Flora flow!

Ah! should Jove but find my fair,
He would fall in love, I swear,
And to his old tricks repair:
   In a cloud of gold descending
     As on Danae's brazen tower,
  Or the sturdy bull's back bending,
     Or would veil his godhood's power
     In a swan's form for one hour.
Oh, the joys of this possessing!
How unspeakable the blessing,
   How divine my Flora's flower!

[J. A. SYMONDS]

The Vow to Cupid

Winter, now thy spite is spent,
Frost and ice and branches bent!
Fogs and furious storms are o'er,
Sloth and torpor, sorrow frore,
Pallid wrath, lean discontent.

Comes the graceful band of May!
Cloudless shines the limpid day,
Shine by night the Pleiades;
While a grateful summer breeze
Makes the season soft and gay.

Golden Love! shine forth to view!
Souls of stubborn men subdue!
See me bend! What is thy mind?
Make the girl thou givest kind,
And a leaping ram's thy due!

O the jocund face of earth,
Breathing with young grassy birth!
Every tree with foliage clad,
Singing birds in greenwood glad,
Flowering fields for lovers' mirth!

[J. A. SYMONDS]

Flowering Time

The time draws near for flowers to spring,
Birds appear and sing and sing,
Earth now comforts everything.
Ah, my dear! well I see
Love has little joy for me.

Not to think of, not to tell—
For a while I hid my fear,
And I loved, I loved too well.
Now my fault must all be clear,
For I feel my body swell;
Childbed and its pangs are near.

For this my mother rates me,
For this my father hates me;
Both do their best to hurt me.
I sit at home outlawed,
I dare not stir abroad,
Nor anywhere divert me.

When in the street I venture out,
People stare that meet me
As if a monster walked about.
Each notes my shape, and judges;
One man another nudges,
And no one cares to greet me.

Nudging elbow so loose-jointed,
Finger always my way pointed,
Am I such a holy show?
Wagging head and curling lip,
Death's too good for me, *you* know,
Just because of one small slip.

Where shall I go, I alone,
I a byword now become
In the mouths of all and some?
What more can I know of grieving
Since my own true love is leaving
Till the storm be overblown?

From my father's countenance
He has fled to farthest France,
Leaving me alone to face
All the gibes, all the disgrace.
In despair I could die,
And I cry and cry and cry.

[GEORGE F. WHICHER]

A Song of Cash

O bring a gift along,
and black soon greys to white.
Cash makes a contract strong,
cash cannot but be right,
cash smoothes the roughest wrong,
cash stops the fiercest fight,
cash in the courts holds sway,
a law that all obey.
Hey, you that judge, I say,
here comes Lord Cash, make way!

Where money talks, the law
soon withers in the din.
The poor folk find the flaw,
though truth is all their sin;
but rich men, priced with awe,
are gently ushered in.
Then down the judge must kneel,
for cash has claimed his zeal.
Cash brings him quick to heel;
he nods, there's no appeal.

When cash upholds the scales,
justice is out of date.
Your crooked business fails?
The court will set it straight.
For cash you'll find prevails
to settle the debate.
Bring nothing, and you'll learn
how quickly courts can spurn.
No cash to serve your turn?
At once the judge is stern.

So courts are made to pay,
the giver gets no hurt.
When money fades away,
the lawyers soon are curt.
All bonds they break today
and daub around their dirt.
Grammar of greed they're taught,
they parse the man that's caught:
tossed (to and from) he's brought
to be a caseless naught.

But do the mighty crowd
to join the lucre-chase?
Though they are much endowed,
not gratis is their grace.
Their blasphemy's avowed:
cash saves the sinner's case.
Not virtue truly wise,
but cash, the clergy prize,
hidden from God's great eyes,
whose angels fill the skies.

Who gives, is given more.
We know the text by rote:
with such an unctuous lore
the saintly villains quote,
and order from the door
the man with ragged coat.
Cash is the bit to jag
the court if it should lag.
Holy the money-bag!
holy the saving swag!

[JACK LINDSAY]

The Sweetness of Spring

Vernal hours are sweet as clover,
With love's honey running over;
Every heart on this earth burning
Finds new birth with spring's returning.

In the spring-time blossoms flourish,
Fields drink moisture, heaven's dews nourish,
Now the griefs of maidens, after
Dark days, turn to love and laughter.

Whoso love, are loved, together
Seek their pastime in spring weather;
And, with time and place agreeing,
Clasp, kiss, frolic, far from seeing.

[J. A. SYMONDS]

Veni Creator Spiritus

Creator Spirit, by whose aid
The world's foundations first were laid,
Come visit ev'ry pious mind;
Come pour thy joys on humankind;
From sin and sorrow set us free,
And make thy temples worthy thee.
     O course of uncreated light,
The Father's promis'd Paraclite!
Thrice holy fount, thrice holy fire,
Our hearts with heav'nly love inspire,
Come, and thy sacred unction bring
To sanctify us, while we sing!

Plenteous of grace, descend from high,
Rich in thy sev'nfold energy,
Thou strength of his almighty hand,
Whose pow'r does heav'n and earth command!
Proceeding Spirit, our defense,
Who dost the gifts of tongues dispense,
And crown'st thy gift with eloquence!
Refine and purge our earthy parts;
But, O, inflame and fire our hearts!
Our frailties help, our vice control,
Submit the senses to the soul;
And when rebellious they are grown,
Then lay thy hand, and hold 'em down.
Chase from our minds th' infernal foe,
And peace, the fruit of love, bestow;
And lest our feet should step astray,
Protect and guide us in the way.
Make us eternal truths receive,
And practice all that we believe:
Give us thyself, that we may see
The Father and the Son, by thee.
Immortal honor, endless fame,
Attend th' Almighty Father's name:
The Saviour Son be glorified,
Who for lost man's redemption died;
And equal adoration be,
Eternal Paraclete, to thee.

[JOHN DRYDEN]

THOMAS OF CELANO (1200?–1255?)

Dies Irae

Day of wrath, the years are keeping,
When the world shall rise from sleeping,
With a clamor of great weeping!

Earth shall fear and tremble greatly
To behold the advent stately
Of the Judge that judgeth straitly.

And the trumpet's fierce impatience
Scatter strange reverberations
Thro' the graves of buried nations.

Death and Nature will stand stricken
When the hollow bones shall quicken
And the air with weeping thicken.

When the Creature, sorrow-smitten,
Rises where the Judge is sitting
And beholds the doom-book written.

For, that so his wrath be slakèd,
All things sleeping shall be wakèd,
All things hidden shall be naked.

When the just are troubled for thee,
Who shall plead for me before thee,
Who shall stand up to implore thee?

Lest my great sin overthrow me,
Let thy mercy, quickened thro' me,
As a fountain overflow me!

For my sake thy soul was movèd;
For my sake thy name reprovèd,
Lose me not whom thou hast lovèd!

Yea, when shame and pain were sorest,
For my love the cross thou borest,
For my love the thorn-plait worest.

By that pain that overbore thee,
By those tears thou weepest for me,
Leave me strength to stand before thee.

For the heart within me yearneth,
And for sin my whole face burneth;
Spare me when thy day returneth.

By the Magdalen forgiven,
By the thief made pure for heaven,
Even to me thy hope was given.

Tho' great shame be heavy on me,
Grant thou, Lord, whose mercy won me,
That hell take not hold upon me.

Thou whom I have lovèd solely,
Thou whom I have lovèd wholly,
Leave me place among the holy!

When thy sharp wrath burns like fire,
With the chosen of thy desire,
Call me to the crownèd choir!

Prayer, like flame with ashes blending,
From my crushed heart burns ascending;
Have thou care for my last ending.
                    [ALGERNON CHARLES SWINBURNE]

Provençal

*O*f the five Romance languages that evolved from the corrupt Latin (called Romanic at the time) as used in the colonies of the Roman Empire, Provençal was the first to refine its vernacular so as to accommodate a great, in fact internationally influential, literature. It did not spring full-blown from a vacuum, however, but was itself influenced by poems and songs of its period. There was first the Latin heritage and beyond that some possible oriental influence, attributable to encounters with Moors and Saracens in crusades and war. There are also verbal and musical derivations from cadences of liturgy and hymns, but especially from native popular songs.

Almost all of the popular songs are lost, but without assuming them and reconstructing from the few in existence, one can hardly conceive of how this brand-new flower of poetry should suddenly blossom. And at the other end of the scale, without this troubadour poetry, one can not conceive of Dante and his school, the Minnesingers, the Trouvères and much other later lyric poetry.

The poems brought to near perfection the type of lyric that was to *continue through the Western World to the present time. Some of the technical achievements had been used before—there were rhymed and accentual poems in Latin, with stanza patterns in variety, and the dance songs of the peasants were doubtless in the same mold—but the Provençal Troubadours refined all the material and added certain inventions of their own.*

*In spite of the charm and beauty of the poems, one is not convinced of the sincerity of personal emotion, unless it is in the sirventes, which dealt in social, political and clerical satire and criticism (see the poems by Cardenal and the Monk of Montaudon). The love poems (*cansos*) are rather artificial and conventional in the matter expressed; their whole admirable quality is in the art of the writing—or the music for which the writing was done. Provençal literature never progressed beyond this first high point in any way during the two centuries of its life.*

The first of the troubadours was Guillem IX of Poitou. Very likely the specimen of his work offered here will not seem to bear out the above remarks about love poems. His other poems are different. They introduce the platonic concept of love—idealized woman, something of a "secularized Virgin Mary" she has been called, who demands the best of the poet while holding rewards to the distant future. His granddaughter, Eleanor of Aquitaine, was an active cultivator of the poets who followed Guillem's trail.

Some 450 troubadours, among them four women, are known by name. Their poems were so much admired that many who felt their own language too crude turned to writing Provençal—among them the Italian Sordello and the Spanish Alfonso II of Aragon. Because the troubadours needed patrons, and the patrons and their ladies needed entertainment, these singers spread far and wide to any hospitable castle or court. With them spread the seeds of their literature, and after Provençal as a creative language had been stamped out by the Albigensian Crusade, the seeds continued to grow. The results are seen in the French Trouvères, the German Minnesingers, and poets of all the provinces of Spain, Portugal and Italy, with traces in England and even Wales.

GUILLEM IX, COUNT OF POITOU (1071–1127)

Poem

I'll write a poem, then sink to dreams
And dwell alone in bright sun beams.
For there are ladies with wicked schemes
    And I know who:
The ones that scorn a cavalier's
    Desire to woo.

A dame in mortal sin is seized
Who loves no loyal knight at least;
But if she loves a monk or priest,
    She's lost her mind:
By right she should be bound and to
    The fire consigned.

Far in Auvergne, past Limousin,
I went alone, disguised, and then
I found the wives of Lords Guarin
    And Bernard there;
They gave me pleasant welcome in
    St. Leonard's square.

One said in dialect to me:
"God save you now, sir pilgrim free;
You seem of quite good family
    By my own rules;
But we see going about the world
    Too many fools."

Now you must hear what I replied:
Never a word did I let slide,
And nothing at all did I confide,
    But stuff to scan:
"Babble-de-boo, babble-de-boo,
    Babble-de-ban."

Then said Dame Ann to Eleanor:
"We've found just whom we're looking for.
For heaven's sake, let's open our door.
    He's dumb as a stone,
And through him never will our tricks
    Be publicly known."

One took me under her vast attire
Into her chamber, near the fire.
She looked inviting, if you inquire,
    And the blaze did grow,
And I was glad to warm myself
    At the embers' glow.

For supper a capon they conveyed,
As no one else was home to aid,
Not cook nor even scullery maid,
    But just we three;
And the bread was white, the wine was strong
    And pepper ran free.

"Now Sister, this man is shrewd, I wage,
And leaves the talk for us to engage;
Let's bring our old red cat from her cage
    Right now and try 'er;
She'll make him talk immediately
    If he's a liar."

Lady Ann then fetched the thing so rash,
And it was huge, with a long mustache;
And when I saw it amidst us dash,
    I feared I would
Most likely lose my courage and
    My hardihood.

When we had drunk and eat our fill,
I doffed my clothes for them to thrill.
Behind they brought the cat whose skill
    Was wicked and mean;
One dragged it down my ribs and thighs
    And even between.

At once by the tail with no delay
She pulled both cat and scratching away:
More than a hundred wounds that day
    Did I sustain;
But still I wouldn't have spoke at all
    Though I were slain.

Then Ann to Lady Eleanor said:
"He *is* mute, plain as eyes in your head;
Sister, get ready for bath and bed
    And dalliance gay."
Eight days thereafter in that furnace
    I had to stay.

How much I tupped them you shall hear:
A hundred eighty-eight times or near,
So that I almost stripped my gear
    And broke my equipment;
I never could list the ills I got—
    Too big a shipment.

I never could list the ills I got—
    Too big a shipment.

                [HUBERT CREEKMORE]

MARCABRUN (*fl.* 1130–1148)

Pastorela

The other day by hedge-row seated,
A shepherdess I found secreted,
Low-born, with joy and wit as needed—
No doubt a peasant's little maid;
With cloak and coat and garments sheeted,
She sat in shift of drill, full-pleated,
And shoes and woolen hose arrayed.

I came across the plain and greeted:
"Maid," I said, "fair thing, ill-treated,
I'm sorry the cold stings unimpeded."
"My lord," thus spake the peasant maid,
"Thank God and my old nurse, well-heeded,
I'd care not if it blew and sleeted;
I'm happy, healthy and unafraid."

"Maiden," I said, "sweet thing, heart-rending,
I've turned off from my road for lending
You company quite comprehending;
For such a helpless peasant maid
Should not, without some nice befriending,
So many animals be tending
In such a country, without aid."

"Dear sir," she said, "birth notwithstanding,
I know both sense and folly's ending;
Your company is good, depending,
My lord," thus spake the peasant maid,
"On whether fit or unoffending;
Those who restraint keep on pretending,
Just seem to have it, to persuade."

"Maiden of such mild condition,
Your father surely was patrician
Who brought your mother such fruition,
For she was a genteel peasant maid.
Each look makes you a fairer vision,
And I'd delight in your decision
To treat me human as I've prayed."

"Sir, all my family and tradition
Belong by endless repetition
To plow and sickle as their mission,
My lord," thus spake the peasant maid;
"Raw knights who want my recognition
Should try a similar position
Six days a week and not evade."

"Maiden," I said, "you gentle fairy,
You got at birth, hereditary,
A beauty most extraordinary
Above all other peasant maids;
Your boon would be twice honorary,
If I just once hugged snugly—very!—
On top with you beneath me laid."

"My lord, you've praised me so unchary,
I'm not annoyed as customary;
You've raised my worth unnecessary,
My lord," thus spake the peasant maid,
"So you'll get this reward to carry
On leaving: useless, fool, to tarry,
Or wait for me at noon in the glade."

"Maid, timid hearts and unrelented
Are tamed by habit, long-frequented.
At sight, I know, if you consented,
With such a pleasant peasant maid
A man could make friends well-contented
With gayest loving ever invented,
If neither one the other betrayed."

"Sir, a man with lust tormented
Swears guarantees unprecedented;
Your praise is all you have presented,
My lord," thus spake the peasant maid;
"But for an entrance fee that's stinted,
I won't trade chastity, so rented,
For the name of prostitute and jade."

"Maid, every being in creation
Must heed its nature's obligation;
For copacetic copulation
We must make ready, peasant maid,
Within the meadow's shelter-station;
For you can have no hesitation
To make this blissful escapade."

"Yes, sir; but by just allocation,
Fools seek their foolish dissipation,
The knight a knightly celebration,
And peasant seeks the peasant maid;
Where wisdom's gone or seems vexation,
A man won't keep to moderation,
So all the ancient folk have said."

"Maid, I've seen no face in the nation
More filled than yours with degradation,
Nor heart with more deception weighed."
"Sir, owls predict from observation:
Some idly gape at simulation,
Some wait the real thing, undismayed."

[HUBERT CREEKMORE]

BERNARD DE VENTADORN (*c.* 1150–95)

No Marvel Is It

No marvel is it if I sing
Better than other minstrels all:
For more than they I am Love's thrall,
And all myself therein I fling,—
Knowledge and sense, body and soul,
And whatso power I have beside;
The rein that doth my being guide
Impels me to this only goal.

His heart is dead whence did not spring
Love's odor, sweet and magical;
His life doth ever on him pall
Who knoweth not that blessed thing;
Yea! God, who doth my life control,
Were cruel did he bid me bide
A month, or even a day, denied
The love whose rapture I extol.

How keen, how exquisite the sting
Of that sweet odor! At its call
An hundred times a day I fall
And faint, an hundred rise and sing.
So fair the semblance of my dole,
'Tis lovelier than another's pride:
If such the ill doth me betide,
Good hap were more than I could thole.

Yet haste, kind heaven! the sundering
True swains from false, great hearts from small!
The traitor in the dust bid crawl!
The faithless to confession bring!
Ah! if I were the master sole
Of all earth's treasures multiplied,
To see my Lady satisfied
Of my pure faith, I'd give the whole.

[HARRIET W. PRESTON]

Canso

I cannot see the bright sun's glow,
So darkened to me is its light,
But this to me gives no affright,
For the fire of love is glowing
In my heart, which it has lightened,
And, though others may be frightened,
I am content, have what I want,
So my song in nought is wanting.

The fields that now are wrapt in snow
Seem to me filled with blossoms bright,
For now my joy is at its height,
And I think, although 'tis snowing,
That the world by spring is brightened.
For my lady-love has heightened
My hopes and said her love she'll grant
—May she ne'er forget the granting!

From fear's advice no good I gain,
'Tis fear that makes the world so bad,
And wicked men, with envy mad,
Strive their purpose to be gaining
—How to make true love fare badly.
Cursèd men who act thus madly,
I would that God would all destroy
Who true love would be destroying!

And of such people I complain
Who make me sorrowful and sad,
For they are grieved when I am glad,
And whene'er they are complaining
And on others' joys look sadly,
I behold their grief right gladly
Since my delight can thus annoy
Those who oft are me annoying.

By night and day I weep and wake
And sigh, but soon I cease to grieve,
And count it joy ills to receive,
For good hope doth gently wake me
And it swiftly cures my grieving;
Sure, 'tis joy I am receiving,
'Tis happiness e'en to desire
Such a love as I'm desiring.

Marvel not, lady, if I take
Such joy in you, but give me leave
To love you; if you do, believe,
Happiness will overtake me,
Grief henceforth I shall be leaving
And all men will be believing
That to a high love I aspire
Since to yours I am aspiring.

[BARBARA SMYTHE]

GIRAUT DE BORNELH (*fl.* 1165–1200)

Canso

When all the ice and cold and snow
Are gone and warm days can resume
And Spring puts on its green costume
And birds are warbling to and fro,
    This gentle show,
With March gone by, I love and crave;
I'm brisk as a lion sprung from cave,
Swifter than deer, gazelle or hare.
If she to whom my troth I swear
    Would crown and bless
Me only enough to acquiesce
That her true lover I might be,
No man could match my treasury.

So blithe and fair her features glow
With perfect tinting and perfume,
That never bloomed a fresher bloom
On rose or any garden row.
     And great Bordeaux
Would never know a lord more brave
Than I, if she received me, gave
Me leave to be her bondsman there;
Yet fool I'm called, with words to spare,
     Since I'll confess
To men no secret I possess
That she told me in secrecy;
Her heart would loathe such perfidy.

Fair one, this ring that you bestow
Gives me great succor in my room;
By it are soothed my pain and gloom,
For when I look, more gay I grow
     Than starlings, though
For you so boldly I behave
That I fear neither lance nor glaive,
And steel nor iron makes me beware.
And even so, more grief I bear
     Through love's excess,
Than ships at sea, whipped in distress,
By wind and wave mauled bitterly;
Thus reels my sweet anxiety.

My lady, as when a strong chateau
Is stormed by mighty knights for whom
Tall engines round the tower loom
And catapult and mangel throw,
     While battles blow
The men all round into the grave,
When no device or ruse can save,
And frightful wails and cries declare
That those inside great anguish share,
     It seems no guess
They must beg mercy none the less;
So mercy is my humble plea,
High lady, full of sympathy.

My lady, as a lamb can show
No strength against a bear, its doom—
Thus I, unless with aid you come,
Am weak as a reed, and faster know
     My life will go;
Its span you'll cut, instead of save,
If all delay you do not waive,
All wrongs to me at once repair.
So you, true Love, who brace me where
     You must suppress
True lovers' acts of foolishness,
My sponsor and defender be
Before my lady, then conquer me!

[HUBERT CREEKMORE]

BERTRAN DE BORN (*fl.* 1180–1200)

Disavowal

I cannot hide from thee how much I fear
The whispers breathed by flatterers in thine ear
Against my faith:—but turn not, oh! I pray,
That heart so true, so faithful, so sincere,
So humble and so frank, to me so dear,
O lady, turn it not from me away!

So may I lose my hawk ere he can spring,
Borne from my hand by some bold falcon's wing,
Mangled and torn before my very eye,
If every word thou utterest does not bring
More joy to me than fortune's favoring,
Or all the bliss another's love might buy!

So with my shield on neck, mid storm and rain,
With vigor blinding me, and shorten'd rein,
With stirrups far too long, so may I ride;
So may my trotting charger give me pain,
So may the ostler treat me with disdain,
As they who tell those tales have grossly lied!

When I approach the gaming board to play,
May I not turn a penny all the day;
Or may the board be shut, the dice untrue,
If the truth dwell not in me when I say,
No other fair e'er wiled my heart away
From her I've long desired and loved—from you!

Or, prisoner to some noble, may I fill
Together with three more, some dungeon chill,
Unto each other odious company;—
Let master, servants, porters, try their skill,
And use me for a target if they will,
If ever I have loved aught else but thee!

So may another knight make love to you,
And so may I be puzzled what to do;
So may I be becalm'd mid oceans wide;
May the king's porters beat me black and blue,
And may I fly ere I the battle view,
As they that slander me have grossly lied!

[EDGAR TAYLOR]

ARNAUT DANIEL (*c.* 1180–1210)

Canso

Softly sighs the April air,
  Ere the coming of the May;
Of the tranquil night aware,
  Murmur nightingale and jay;
Then, when dewy dawn doth rise,
  Every bird in his own tongue
Wakes his mate with happy cries;
  All their joy abroad is flung.

Gladness, lo! is everywhere
  When the first leaf sees the day;
And shall I alone despair,
  Turning from sweet love away?
Something to my heart replies,
  Thou too wast for rapture strung;
Wherefore else the dreams that rise
  Round thee when the year is young?

One, than Helen yet more fair,
  Loveliest blossom of the May,
Rose-tints hath and sunny hair,
  And a gracious mien and gay;
Heart that scorneth all disguise,
  Lips where pearls of truth are hung,—
God, who gives all sovereignties,
  Knows her like was never sung.

Though she lead through long despair,
  I would never say her nay,
If one kiss—reward how rare!—
  Each new trial might repay.
Swift returns I'd then devise,
  Many labors, but not long.
Following so fair a prize
  I could nevermore go wrong.

[HARRIET W. PRESTON]

THE MONK OF MONTAUDON (*fl.* 1180–1215)

Vexational

Much vexes me; you'll hear my recital?
The gabby man whose pledge is idle
and the man who's much too homicidal
annoy, and steeds that pull on bridle;
I'm vexed, God help me, and unstrung
by a youth whose shield is always slung
but never a blow against it rung;
by priest and monk with whiskers hung,
and gossips with a cutting tongue.

I find a woman most vexatious
when poor but stuck-up and ungracious;
a man with wife he loves tenacious
though she's from Toulouse and loquacious;
and I don't like the knight effete
who boasts outside his country seat,
and yet at home no charge can meet
except in bowls to grind and beat
the pepper or keep the fireplace neat.

I'm vexed as by a stinging nettle
by cowards waving flags with mettle;
by hunting hawks in sorry fettle,
by skimpy meat in a mammoth kettle;
I hate, by good St. Martin's sign,
a pint of water drowning my wine!
To meet the lame in morning-shine
annoys, and blind men I decline
because their way does not suit mine.

Long abstinence I've always hated,
and meat cooked hard, almost cremated,
a lying priest with vows violated,
an old whore who won't die, though fated;
and by St. Delmas, I despise
a vile man heaped with joy through vice;
to run when roads are caked with ice;
to flee on horseback, armed, is twice
as grim, and oaths of men at dice.

By eternal life, it's sorely smarting
to dine fireless with snowflakes darting,
to sleep with some old tart whose farting
brings tavern smells in her bombarding;
it's vexing and too foul a lot
to ask the drab to wash my pot;
I hate a husband rough and hot
when I've seen that cute wife he's got
and she won't offer me a jot.

By Holy God, I ever detested
a sorry fiddler in fine court nested,
a small estate with heirs infested,
fast poker by stingy bets arrested;
and by St. Martial, I hate like pain
one mantle with fur linings twain,
too many peers in one domain,
rich lords who seldom entertain,
and bows and darts on tourney-plain.

I hate, Lord help me hold my spittle,
large tables spread with cloths too little,
a scabby lackey carving victuals,
a gross hauberk of mail that's brittle;
I hate to wait outside the door
when weather's bad and showers pour;
to be with friends who wrangle and roar
is vexing, and I suffer more
to know they're wrong on every score.

I'll tell now what annoys unended:
an old slut too made-up and mended,
a poor jade feigning she's offended,
a youth admiring his legs as splendid;
by St. Abundus, I hate with gall
a soft fat dame with slot too small;
bad lords who fleece their serfs appall,
but what I hate most to befall
is, when I'm sleepy, no sleep at all.

Indeed there's more that's very paining:
to ride with no cloak when it's raining,
to find a sow with my horse, draining
his trough of all the grain remaining;
and these I hate, and end my song:
a saddle with wobbly horn, not strong,
a buckle that has lost its prong,
and a wicked man at home day-long
who can't behave or speak but wrong.

[HUBERT CREEKMORE]

PEIRE CARDENAL (*c*. 1225–72)

Sirventes

The paramours, to those who would accuse,
defend themselves as lightly as they may:
one takes a man since born to noble views,
another since her poverty might slay,
one says she's young and with a graybeard's lying,
one's huge and keeps a tiny popinjay,
one has no woolen cloak but soon she's buying,
and one has two, but does it anyway.

He's close to war who's got one running loose—
closer, if one should lie abed all day;
when husband vexes wife, right then there brews
a war much worse than any neighbors' fray;
I know one who, when from Toledo hieing,
hears not his sister, wife nor mother pray
in faith: "God send him back to stop my sighing!"
But once he's gone, the saddest shouts Hurray!

She'll serve a feast, but no respect ensues,
who kills a stolen steer or one astray;
I know someone whose kettle's full of stews
at Christmas-time, but names I won't betray;
such meat's not wholesome and there's no denying
it's banned and breaks the laws we should obey;
simpler than sucking babe that needs a drying
is he who thinks it honors Christmas day.

If some poor fellow steals a sheet to use,
he's branded thief and crushed with deep dismay;
a rich man steals quicksilver by the cruse
but outwits Constantine[1] and need not pay;
poor thieves for but a ribbon hang there dying,
and those who stole a nag from gallows sway;
our justice is more just than arrows flying
when rich thief hangs poor thief in such fair play.

I sing and play my lute just as I choose,
since none can fathom what my rimes may say;
no more than thoughts of nightingales from coos,
do people grasp the thought my songs convey;
I don't know Dutch or Breton speechifying,
can't speak the Flemish or the Anjou way;
but evil, when a charge of guilt is crying,
blinds everyone to truth with its decay.

It's just too bad for me a dolt is trying
to sing my song; he gives a donkey's bray.

[HUBERT CREEKMORE]

[1] i.e., the laws of Constantine.

French

*P*oetry in French, the language spoken in the north of France as opposed to the Provençal of the south, entered upon the literary scene at an early date with long religious works, secular epics and narrative poems. The lyrical outbursts of the southern Troubadours had an immediate effect on French poets, though to some extent the courtly love poem was a spontaneous development in both these closely related regions. Anonymous songs, called chansons de toile because they were sung by women while sewing and embroidering, were of popular origin. They describe dramas of love, seeming to condense more elaborate romances, in much the same way that strict ballads were to do later.

Love, in fact, was very much in the air, but with attributes it never had in classical writings. The drama of Tristan and Isolde would have been inconceivable to an ancient Greek or Roman. A romanticized conception of love, which is still overpoweringly with us, was being created in poets by the feudal society and the Christian mentality of the Middle Ages. Beginning with the Provençal image of the noble unattainable lady—a most satisfactory idea, socially, since it provided *inspiration for song and entertainment in the court, and at the same time protected against infidelity—the love theme became increasingly mystical, fusing ideals of chivalric honor with Christian aesceticism, and rising to more exquisite heights the more obstacles arose to thwart its fulfillment. The conventional, even artificial, character of the poem's substance should not be taken to mean that none of the poems were evoked by real emotion.*

Among the many Trouvères—French counterparts of the Troubadours—of the twelfth and thirteenth centuries, Thibaut of Champagne is perhaps the finest, though many would argue for the Chatelain of Coucy or others impossible to include here. Luckily, all the poetry did not aim at their exalted elegance—one might have become bored with so much sweet frustration, or might have despaired for the continuance of the human race.

French literature, like all medieval literatures, had its scoffers, humorists, satirists and angry writers. The crude, hearty, often bawdy quality of these poets is a needed contrast to the yearnings of the love poets. Though Conon de Béthune wrote courtly lyrics, he could also make fun of the convention, by carrying the unattainable lady to a ridiculously logical conclusion. Colin Muset wrote love songs, as a professional minstrel, but he could also describe bitingly the hazards of that life. Rutebeuf offered an even grimmer view of the plight of the penniless poet, and elsewhere mirrored truly the life of his times.

Early in the fourteenth century the spirit of literature drooped and the attitudes and forms—ballade, rondeau and virelay were French inventions—became even more sterile. Two outstanding exceptions— Charles d'Orléans and Villon—were gifted with excellent techniques for refurbishing the old forms, and with extraordinary, strong personalities and mental qualities. In substance and tone, however, the poems that came from those similar traits are quite different.

PHILIPPE DE THAON (*fl.* 1121–35)

The Unicorn

Monoceros, beast that's born
With on its head one horn
From which it hath a name,
Is like a goatlet in frame.
By a virgin it is caught;
Now hear how this is wrought:
If men would hunt it as prey
And catch and take it away,
Into the forest they hie
Where its deep haunt doth lie;
And there a virgin is placed,
Her breast outside her waist;
And by the fragrance about,
Monoceros smells her out.
He then to the virgin wends,
Kisses her breast and bends
To fall asleep on them,
Thus cometh his death to him.
At once the men up-leap
And slay it while it sleeps,
Or catch it alive and fit,
And do as they will with it.
Great meaning doth this contain,
I'll stop not till I explain.
Monoceros is the Greek:
One horn, the way we speak.
A beast of might so prized
Doth signify Jesus Christ:
Our Lord it is and will stay,
Was and will be for aye;
In the Virgin he began
And put on flesh for man,
And pure virginity;

As proof of chastity,
To the Virgin he appeared
And him she conceived, revered:
Virgin she is, was, will be
And will stay eternally.
Now briefly give your ear
To the signification here.
In truth this animal thus
Represents God to us;
The Virgin then represents
Saint Mary, you know, and hence
By her breast is understood
The church, holy and good.
And peace is what the kiss
Must signify in all this.
And man, when he goeth to sleep,
The feint of death doth keep:
Like unto man slept God
Who suffered death on the rood;
And went unto death's prince.
His death was died long since:
To us his destruction gave
Salvation from the grave,
And his travail and pain
Our repose and ease did gain.
So God the devil deceived
By semblance fitly achieved.
The devil deceives man a lot;
God-man, whom he knows not,
Deceives the devil thus
By virtue meet and decorous:
As soul and flesh are man
So this was God and man.
And this is what signifies
The beast of such might and prize.

[RICHARD BEAUMONT]

ANONYMOUS CHANSONS DE TOILE
(12th century)

*Fair Erembor**

When comes in May, with what we call long hours,
When Franks of France are met the King before,
Reynaut was there among the foremost powers.
He, passing by the house of Erembor,
Deign'd not to raise his head unto the tower.
   Eh, Reynaut, my friend!

Fair Erembor, who at the window there
Held on her knees a stuff of color'd thread,
Saw how the Franks did to the Court repair,
And Reynaut who so haughtily him bare.
She lifted up her voice and these words said:—
   "Eh, Reynaut, my friend!"

"Friend Reynaut! I ere this have seen the hour
That, passing underneath my father's tower,
Thou wast in dole except I spoke to thee."
"Thou hast ill done, daughter of the Emperor!
Another thou hast loved, forgotten me."
   Eh, Reynaut, my friend!

"Sire Reynaut! I will make me clear of this:
Unto a hundred virgins I will swear,
And thirty dames bring with me to declare
Before the Saints none else my lover is.
Take the amend, and I your lips will kiss."
   Eh, Reynaut, my friend!

The county Reynaut mounted up the stair.
Broad-shoulder'd he, but by the bauldric slim,
Blond-featured, all in little curls his hair.
In no land was a bachelor so fair;
And Erembor 'gan weep beholding him.
          Eh, Reynaut, my friend!

The county Reynaut is within her bower,
And seated on a bed with many a flower
Be-painted; the fair Erembor is fain:
          *   *   *
Then did their early loves begin again.
          Eh, Reynaut, my friend!

[W. J. LINTON]

* The omitted line in the last stanza has not been censored; it is lost from
the manuscripts.

Poor Me

Why does my husband beat me?
Poor me, I brood.

For I've done nothing wrong to him,
No scandal caused or done by whim,
But hug my sweet friend limb to limb
      In solitude.
Why does my husband beat me?
Poor me, I brood.

If he won't let me go my way
Leading a merry life in play,
I'll see he's called a cuckold today
      For sure, the prude!
Why does my husband beat me?
Poor me, I brood.

I now know what I'll do—it's clear—
And how I'll get revenge right here:
I'll go to bed with my lover dear,
      A wee bit nude.
Why does my husband beat me?
Poor me, I brood.

[RICHARD BEAUMONT]

Three Sisters

Three sisters by the sea side
Sing clear and bright:
The youngest was brunette:
"Of a dark-haired friend I know—
I've got brown hair,
I'll have a brown-haired friend also."

Three sisters by the sea side
Sing clear and bright:
The one born second calls
To Robin her dear swain:
"You took me in the leafy woods,
Take me there again."

Three sisters by the sea side
Sing clear and bright:
The oldest said:
"He should love a damoselle
And her love guard well
Who has it now."

[RICHARD BEAUMONT]

ANONYMOUS (12th century)

Song

Would you wish me to sing to you
Song of love no villein knew,
    Song of many charms?
For a knight this singing made
Lying neath an olive's shade
    In his lady's arms.

Linen was her small camise,
White with ermine her pelisse,
    She had a silken gown.
Tiger lilies were her hose,
Flowers o' may her little shoes,
    Fitted tightly on.

For a girdle, tender leaves,
When the weather rained, grew green,
    Buttoned up with gold.
Cords of flowers swung above
Her wallet shapen all for love,
    And Love the giver bold.

On a mule she rode along,
And the mule was silver shod,
    Saddle gold inlaid;
On the crupper right behind,
Three rose trees stood up in line
    For to give her shade.

She went riding through the mead;
All the knights who met her steed
    Bowed with courtly state.
"Lady fair, whence are you sped?"
"I am the boast of France," she said,
    "Of renowned estate."

"My father is the nightingale
Who sings within the bosky dale
    On the tallest tree.
The mermaiden my mother is,
Who sings her melodies
    In the deep salt sea."

"Lady, blessed was your birth,
Parentage of famous worth
    And renowned estate.
Would that God our Father dear
Gave you for to be my peer
    And my wedded mate."

                    [CLAUDE C. ABBOTT]

Encounter

Upon the first new morn of May
From Paris out I rode to play
As one with heart in piteous plight
All for his cruel love's despite.
Aloud I heard a voice to sing,
A lady fain of love seemed she,
"My father did no courteous thing
Who to a villein married me."

Soon as the lady's plaint I heard
I went to her, spake her this word,
"Lady, God save your body fair,
Why is it that you weep so there?"
She said to me, "Sir knight, pardie,
My traitor man has me betrayed.
My father did not courteously
Who married me to such a knave."

"Dame, never will I lie to you:
I have a loving heart and true.
And I will serve you soon and late
As your sweet lover dedicate
Without offence or treachery."
"Fair Sir, I give you my love's joy,
My heart doth own your mastery
And seeks no other fond employ."

Hot-foot I ran to clip her round
And threw her on the grassy ground.
Three times I did her without stay
Desport that men call lovers' way.
She said to me, "Sweet lover true,
My husband never, day or night,
Did so to me, I warrant you,
For this my love is your delight."

With great delight and much content
She spoke to me, with sweet intent,
"My love, do it to me again."
Without delay began I then
To busy me the way she bade.
Right mad I was when I could not.
"Now by my faith, sir knight," she said,
"You are a very niggard sot.

"'Tis mockery to lie me down
With man but is a boasting clown.
False coward heart, away from here,
At an old drum you were too dear,
A worthy dame is shamed for aye
Who gives her love to such a one."
"Certes, lady, and what care I?
Who plucks the flower, his work is done."

[CLAUDE C. ABBOTT]

THE CHATELAIN OF COUCY (d. 1203)

Chanson

My wand'ring thoughts awake to love anew,
  And bid me rise to sing the fairest fair
That e'er before the world of beauty knew,
  That e'er kind Nature made her darling care:
And when, entranced, on all her charms I muse,
All themes but that alone my days refuse,
Each wish my soul can form is hers alone,
My heart, my joys, my feelings all her own!

Since first my trembling heart became a prey,
  I have no power to turn me back again;
At once I yield me to that passion's sway,
  Nor idly seek its impulse to restrain.
If she, who is all sweetness, truth, and joy,
Were cold and fickle, were she proud or coy,
I might my tender hopes at once resign,
But not, thank heaven! so sad a lot is mine!

If aught I blame 'tis my hard fate alone,
  Not those soft eyes, those gentle looks of thine,
On which I gazed till all my peace was gone!
  Not at their dear perfection I repine,
I cannot blame that form all winning grace,
That fairy hand, that lip, that lovely face;
All I can beg is that she love me more,
That I may live still longer to adore!

Yes, all I ask of thee, oh lady dear,
  Is but what purest love may hope to find;
And if thine eyes, whose crystal light so clear
  Reflect thy thoughts, be not to me unkind.
Well may'st thou see, by ev'ry mournful lay,
By all I ever look, or sigh, or say,
That I am thine, devoted to thy will,
And, midst my sadness, fondly thank thee still.

I thank thee, even for these secret sighs,
  For all the mournful thoughts that on thee dwell,
For as thou bad'st them in my bosom rise,
  Thou canst revive their sweetest hopes as well,
The blissful remedy for all my woe
In those dear eyes, that gentle voice I know;
Should Fate forbid my soul to love thee more,
My life, alas! would with my grief be o'er.

To thee my heart, my wishes I resign,
I am thine own, oh lady dear, be mine!
                  [LOUISA S. COSTELLO]

CONON DE BÉTHUNE (d. 1220)

Too Late, My Love

Once on a time it happened that a knight
Had loved a lady—'twas in other land—,
And while she was possessed of beauty still
Her love to him she had forbid and banned.
Then came an hour she whispered to him, "Dear,
With words I have allured you, many a day;
Now is your love both recognized and proved.
Henceforward I am wholly in your sway."

The knight looked then upon her countenance
And saw how pale she was and wan of hue,
"Lady," said he, "I am unfortunate
That long ago this thought came not to you.
Your radiant face, that like the lily shone,
Has drooped and withered, lady, more and more;
Now is it plain that you are not for me,
Too late this resolution opes the door."

And when the lady heard this raillery
She was ashamed by it, and foolish sped,
"Vassal, pardie, I spoke it you to mock,
Did you believe it was the truth I said?
There never was a day when I thought thus.
How love a noble dame, could you know this?
Never, pardie, 'tis rather your delight
To have a pretty boy to coll and kiss."

"Lady," said he, "I have indeed heard tell
About your worth, but that was not of late;
And I have listened while men talked of Troy,
How once she was of marvelous estate;
Now one can find but ruins in that place.
And yet you would explain the matter thus
That all shall be accused of knavery
Who are not of your favor curious."

"Vassal, pardie, it was great foolishness
To think you might reproach me with my age.
What though my youth I had used wholly up,
Yet am I rich and of such lineage
A little for my look men love me still.
And scarcely has a month entirely past
Since Monferrat sent me his messenger,
And for my love Des Barres broke a lance."

"Lady, pardie, it is your grievous hurt
That always to exalted rank you cling;
A hundred such may once have sighed for you
Who nevermore will ask you anything
Though you were daughter of the Carthage King.
A lady is not loved for her degree
But when she's wise and courteous and fair.
You will discover soon that verity."

[CLAUDE C. ABBOTT]

THIBAUT OF CHAMPAGNE (1201–1253)

Chanson

There is no comfort to be found for pain
Save only where the heart has made its home.
Therefore I can but murmur and complain
Because no comfort to my pain has come
From where I garnered all my happiness.
From true love have I only earned distress
      The truth to say.
Grace, Lady! give me comfort to possess
      A hope one day.

Seldom the music of her voice I hear
Or wonder at the beauty of her eyes.
It grieves me that I may not follow there
Where at her feet my heart attentive lies.
Oh, gentle Beauty without consciousness,
Let me once feel a moment's hopefulness,
      If but one ray!
Grace, Lady! give me comfort to possess
      A hope one day.

Certain there are who blame upon me throw
Because I will not tell whose love I seek;
But truly, lady, none my thought may know,
None that is born, save you to whom I speak
In cowardice and awe and doubtfulness,
That you may happily with fearlessness
      My heart essay.
Grace, Lady! give me comfort to possess
      A hope one day.

                    [HENRY ADAMS]

Chanson: Leaving on Crusade

Ah, gentle lady! must I go,
　And quit this sweet, enchanting shore,
Where I, 'tis true, have suffered woe,
　But, thus to leave thee, suffer more.
Why, cruel Nature, didst thou frame
　A land from bliss so far removed,
Where joy exists but as a name,
　And banish'd is each dream of love?
Without affection can I live?
　'Tis all my solace, all my thought,
My heart can nought beside receive,
　For me with vital breath 'tis fraught.
I learnt to prize it in a school,
　Where too severe my lessons were,
Ever to grow content or cool,
　Or weary absence strive to bear.
Do I deserve this life of care?
　My truth methinks thou must approve,
Who art the purest, brightest fair,
　That ever man durst ask to love!
Alas! if I must leave thee so,
　What ceaseless torments will be mine,
When, but an hour condemn'd to go,
　My fainting heart would still repine!
If now I tear myself from thee,
　Will not remorse, regret, betide,
When thy dear lines with tears I see,
　And know what seas our fates divide!
Oh Heaven! be thine my future days,—
　Farewell each hope that bade me live,—
Rich the reward thy hand displays,
　To thee my love, my joy, I give.

See, in thy service I prepare,
  My fortunes henceforth are thy own,
I seek thy banner, blest and fair,
  Who serves thee ne'er can be o'erthrown.
My bosom throbs 'twixt joy and pain,
  For grief that from my love I part:
For joy that I shall now maintain
  His cause, whose glory nerves my heart.
The love of Heaven is ever blest,
  Without all shade or taint of harm,
A gem, how precious when possest!
  Which all the sins of earth can charm.
Bright queen, and lady without peer!
  To guard me be thy power display'd:
Fill thou my soul with faith sincere,
  I lose my lady—lady, aid!

[LOUISA S. COSTELLO]

COLIN MUSET (13th century)

Complaint of the Minstrel's Life

My lord, within thy halls I've stayed,
And on my lute before thee played,
But naught for wages hast thou paid
To one who plied for thee his trade.
      'Tis villeiny!
Now, by my faith in Saint Marie,
No more thy follower I'll be.
An ill-found satchel here 's to see,
And a purse lean through poverty.

My lord, come, let thy heart persuade
Thy will to grant to me some aid,
For, sire, a gift that's freely made,
A generous gift not long delayed,
  Marks high degree.
Trust me, I purpose verily
To travel home to my country.
If I return with purse empty,
My wife will have no smile for me.

In words like these hear her upbraid:
Sir Starveling, where can you have stayed,
Who not a penny-piece have made?
Too long about some town you've strayed
  In revelry.
Limp saddlebags you bring to me,
For stuffed with naught but wind they be.
Oh, what a shameless wretch is he
Who'ld travel in your company!

But when I'm home, and undismayed
My wife has all my load surveyed,
Fat saddlebags behind me laid
And me in good grey cloth arrayed,
  Such finery,
She flings her distaff down in glee;
She cannot hide her ecstasy,
But laughs at me for jollity
And round my neck clings lovingly.

For joy her work is not delayed,
Straps are unloosed, my stuff displayed;
My man has watered well my jade,
And rubbed her down, ere word is said;
Two capons from the yard my maid
Has killed and cooked, and ready laid
        So savoury;
My daughter out of courtesy
Has brought in hand a comb for me.
So I'm at home His Majesty
In undisturbed felicity;
Say, can a man so happy he?

                              [J. G. LEGGE]

MARIE DE FRANCE (13th century)

Song from Chartivel

Hath any loved you well, down there,
    Summer or winter through?
Down there, have you found any fair
    Laid in the grave with you?
Is death's long kiss a richer kiss
    Than mine was wont to be—
Or have you gone to some far bliss
    And quite forgotten me?

What soft enamoring of sleep
  Hath you in some soft way?
What charmed death holdeth you with deep
  Strange lure by night and day?
A little space below the grass,
  Out of the sun and shade;
But worlds away from me, alas,
  Down there where you are laid.

My brightest waved and wasted gold,
  What is it now to thee—
Whether the rose-red life I hold
  Or white death holdeth me?
Down there you love the grave's own green,
  And evermore you rave
Of some sweet seraph you have seen
  Or dreamt of in the grave.

There you shall lie as you have lain,
  Though in the world above,
Another live your life again,
  Loving again your love:
Is it not sweet beneath the palm?
  Is it not warm day rife
With some long mystic golden calm
  Better than love and life?

The broad quaint odorous leaves like hands
  Weaving the fair day through,
Weave sleep no burnished bird withstands,
  While death weaves sleep for you;
And many a strange rich breathing sound
  Ravishes morn and noon:
And in that place you must have found
  Death a delicious swoon—

Hold me no longer for a word
   I used to say or sing:
Ah, long ago you must have heard
   So many a sweeter thing:
For rich earth must have reached your heart
   And turned the faith to flowers;
And warm wing stolen, part by part,
   Your soul through faithless hours.

And many a soft seed must have won
   Soil of some yielding thought,
To bring a bloom up to the sun
   That else had ne'er been brought;
And, doubtless, many a passionate hue
   Hath made that place more fair,
Making some passionate part of you
   Faithless to me down there.

               [ARTHUR O'SHAUGHNESSY]

RUTEBEUF (*fl.* 1250–1285)

The Poet's Poverty

Where to begin I do not know;
Such are the stories of grief that grow
As I recount my misery.
True King of France, in God's name give
The wherewithal a man may live;
So wilt thou show great charity.
I've lived on gifts of other men,
Loans that they thought I'd pay again.
At last no credit have I left,
All know I'm poor and deep in debt;
And since abroad thy course is set,
Of my sole hope I'm now bereft.

Hard times and this my family—
Of healthy appetite they be—
Leave naught on which to raise a loan.
Before me people shut the door,
In art of giving scant their lore,
Though all well-schooled to guard their own.
Death has made havoc of my friends,
And thou, good king, for pious ends,
Hast swept my patrons far from me
In two crusades to distant lands,
Where Tunis, savage waste of sands,
Rears an ill brood in heresy.

Great king, if I should fail with thee,
I've failed with all, no fault in me!
Food fails me, and for food I fail.
None grips my hand, I've nought to pawn;
From cold I cough, from hunger yawn,
Both ills my tortured frame assail.
I've neither coverlet nor bed,
Far as Senlis none so ill-fed;
Sire, I know not what way to go.
How the hard straw my sides doth gall!
A bed of straw's no bed at all,
And I've for bed but straw to strow.

Sire, take to heart what I have said,
I've nothing left to buy me bread:
Round me in Paris men have all,
But naught is mine to cheer my soul.
Paulatim comes some meager dole,
Which make me think more of St. Paul
Than all the other saintly powers.
Our Father! ay, but is he ours,
When these hard times have ruined me,
And have my lodging so bereft
I've neither creed nor credit left?
I've nothing but what you can see. [J. G. LEGGE]

JEAN FROISSART (1337?–1405?)

Virelay

Too long it seems e'er I shall view
The maid so gentle, fair, and true,
　　Whom loyally I love:
Ah! for her sake, where'er I rove,
　　All scenes my care renew!
I have not seen her—ah, how long!
Nor heard the music of her tongue;
Though in her sweet and lovely mien
Such grace, such witchery is seen,
　　Such precious virtues shine,
My joy, my hope is in her smile,
And I must suffer pain the while,
Where once all bliss was mine.
　　Too long it seems!
Oh tell her, love!—the truth reveal,
Say that no lover yet could feel
　　Such sad consuming pain:
While banish'd from her sight I pine,
And still this wretched life is mine,
　　Till I return again.
She must believe me, for I find
So much her image haunts my mind,
　　So dear her memory,
That wheresoe'er my steps I bend,
The form my fondest thoughts attend,
　　Is present to my eye.
　　　Too long it seems!

Now tears my weary hours employ,
Regret and thoughts of sad annoy,
   When waking or in sleep,
For hope my former care repaid,
In promises at parting made,
   Which happy love might keep.
Oh for one hour my truth to tell,
To speak of feelings known too well,
   Of hopes too vainly dear;
But useless are my anxious sighs,
Since fortune my return denies,
   And keeps me ling'ring here:
     Too long it seems!

                    [LOUISA S. COSTELLO]

CHRISTINE DE PISAN (c. 1363–1430)

If Frequently to Mass

If frequently to mass I go,
My beauty there I fain would see;
Fresh as a new-blown rose is she.

Men waste their time who gossip so;
Why should they talk maliciously,
If frequently to mass I go?

Nor road nor path my footsteps know,
Save one that leads where she may be.
How foolish he who fool calls me,
If frequently to mass I go.

                    [J. G. LEGGE]

CHARLES D'ORLÉANS

Rondel to his Mistress

Strengthen, my Love, this castle of my heart,
   And with some store of pleasure give me aid,
For Jealousy, with all them of his part,
   Strong siege about the weary tower has laid.
   Nay, if to break his bands thou art afraid,
Too weak to make his cruel force depart,
Strengthen at least this castle of my heart,
   And with some store of pleasure give me aid.
Nay, let not Jealousy, for all his art
   Be master, and the tower in ruin laid,
   That still, ah Love! thy gracious rule obeyed.
Advance, and give me succour of thy part;
Strengthen, my Love, this castle of my heart.

[ANDREW LANG]

Rondeau of Spring

We'll to the woods and gather may
Fresh from the footprints of the rain;
   We'll to the woods, at every vein
To drink the spirit of the day.
The winds of the spring are out at play,
   The needs of spring in heart and brain.
We'll to the woods and gather may
   Fresh from the footprints of the rain.
The world's too near her end, you say?—
   Hark to the blackbird's mad refrain.
   It waits for her, the vast Inane?—
Then, girls, to help her on the way
We'll to the woods and gather may.

[W. E. HENLEY]

Rondeau—The Well

The deep well of my Melancholy
That ever on Hope's water draws,
A thirst for Comfort calls with force
Although I often find it dry.

At times I see it clear and free,
At times a troubled, muddy source,
The deep well of my Melancholy
That ever on Hope's water draws.

My ink I dip there, studiously,
To write of it;—but then to cross
Me, Fortune comes to rend my verse
And casts all down, in enmity,
The deep well of my Melancholy.

[BARBARA HOWES]

Ballade Written during Captivity in England

Gazing upon the distant land of France,
It happened that, at Dover on the sea,
The thought came back to me by some mischance
Of joys I'd known there once when I was free:
And I began to sigh most bitterly,
Although, 'tis true, great bliss it did impart
To see sweet France that holds my loving heart.

And then I bade my heart to look askance
On unavailing sighs heaved foolishly,
Perpending that pourparlers held a chance
Of peace, that could all blessings bring to me.
Then sang my thought consolingly.
Yet ceased I not, though comfort eased the smart,
To see sweet France that holds my loving heart.

Then begged I Hope, good ship, to hasten hence
With all my wishes laden, so that she
Might cross the sea and straightway unto France
Make known my dear desires commendingly.
Now give us, God, a good peace speedily,
That, if 'tis fated so, I may depart
To see sweet France that holds my loving heart.

Peace cannot be extollèd fittingly,
And, right or wrong, I hate War, for 'tis he
Confines me here, unable—dearest smart—
To see sweet France that holds my loving heart.

[ALAN CONDER]

Ballade—The Hostelry of Thought

Across the forest of Delay,
By many a winding woodland route,
This present year, full eagerly,
Drawn by desire have I set out.
The aides that I despatched have sought
To find me lodging in the city
Of Destiny, and take what ought
To satisfy my heart and me,
The goodly hostelry of Thought.

And I have marshalled forty bay
Steeds, for my officers have brought
Sixty or more all told—pray
God!—and baggage-mules to boot.
If inns be wanting or all bought
Up, we will scatter readily;
Yet be it only for one night,
Whatever comes, I will essay
The goodly hostelry of Thought.

My ready funds I spend each day
In actions of some daring sort,
The which a jealous Fate who plays
Me cruelly takes in ill part.
But if my Hopes run high and straight,
And hold to what they promised me,
Such seasoned troops will I have wrought
I'll win, despite my enemy,
The goodly hostelry of Thought.

Prince, true heavenly deity,
Your grace I pray be my resort,
Until what I desire I see—
The goodly hostelry of Thought.

[BARBARA HOWES]

FRANÇOIS VILLON (1431?–1489?)

His Mother's Service to Our Lady

Lady of Heaven and earth, and therewithal
   Crowned Empress of the nether clefts of Hell,—
I, thy poor Christian, on thy name do call,
   Commending me to thee, with thee to dwell,
   Albeit in nought I be commendable.
But all mine undeserving may not mar
Such mercies as thy sovereign mercies are;
   Without the which (as true words testify)
No soul can reach thy Heaven so fair and far.
   Even in this faith I choose to live and die.

Unto thy Son say thou that I am His,
   And to me graceless make Him gracious.
Sad Mary of Egypt lacked not of that bliss,
   Nor yet the sorrowful clerk Theophilus,
   Whose bitter sins were set aside even thus
Though to the Fiend his bounden service was.
Oh help me, lest in vain for me should pass
   (Sweet Virgin that shalt have no loss thereby!)
The blessed Host and sacring of the Mass.
   Even in this faith I choose to live and die.

A pitiful poor woman, shrunk and old,
   I am, and nothing learn'd in letter-lore.
Within my parish-cloister I behold
   A painted Heaven where harps and lutes adore,
   And eke an Hell whose damned folk seethe full sore:
One bringeth fear, the other joy to me.
That joy, great Goddess, make thou mine to be,—
   Thou of whom all must ask it even as I;
And that which faith desires, that let it see.
   Even in this faith I choose to live and die.

O excellent Virgin Princess! thou didst bear
King Jesus, the most excellent comforter,
Who even of this our weakness craved a share
And for our sake stooped to us from on high,
Offering to death His young life sweet and fair.
Such as He is, Our Lord, I Him declare,
And in this faith I choose to live and die.

[D. G. ROSSETTI]

Epistle in Form of a Ballad to His Friends

Have pity, pity, friends, have pity on me,
Thus much at least, may it please you, of your grace!
I lie not under hazel or hawthorn-tree
Down in this dungeon ditch, mine exile's place
By leave of God and fortune's foul disgrace.
Girls, lovers, glad young folk and newly wed,
Jumpers and jugglers, tumbling heel o'er head,
Swift as a dart, and sharp as needle-ware,
Throats clear as bells that ring the kine to shed,
Your poor old friend, what, will you leave him there?

Singers that sing at pleasure, lawlessly,
Light, laughing, gay of word and deed, that race
And run like folk light-witted as ye be
And have in hand nor current coin nor base,
Ye wait too long, for now he's dying apace.
Rhymers of lays and roundels sung and read,
Ye'll brew him broth too late when he lies dead.
Nor wind nor lightning, sunbeam nor fresh air,
May pierce the thick wall's bound where lies his bed;
Your poor old friend, what, will you leave him there?

O noble folk, from tithes and taxes free,
　　Come and behold him in this piteous case,
Ye that nor king nor emperor holds in fee,
　　But only God in heaven; behold his face
　　Who needs must fast, Sundays and holidays,
Which makes his teeth like rakes; and when he hath fed
With never a cake for banquet but dry bread,
　　Must drench his bowels with much cold watery fare,
With board nor stool, but low on earth instead;
　　Your poor old friend, what, will you leave him there?

Princes afore-named, old and young foresaid,
Get me the king's seal and my pardon sped,
　　And hoist me in some basket up with care:
So swine will help each other ill bested,
For where one squeaks they run in heaps ahead,
　　Your poor old friend, what, will you leave him there?
                                    [ALGERNON CHARLES SWINBURNE]

Ballade of the Hanged Men

Men and brothers, who after us shall be,
Let not your hearts too hard against us grow,
For if on us poor men you take pity,
God will be merciful to you also.
You see us, five or six, hung in a row,
That flesh we too much fattened long ago
Now tattered, eaten off, a rotten dough;
And we, the bones, are growing pulverous.
Our wretchedness let no one laugh to see,
But pray God's mercy upon all of us.

If brother men you are, you need not be
Scornful of us, though Justice as I know
Cut short our lives. You know as well as we,
All men cannot be steady here below.
Forgive us, since we are transported so
To Mary's son, to kneel at his elbow,
And never may his fount of grace run low,
From thunderclap of Hell preserving us.
We are dead now, and mind no misery,
Yet pray God's mercy upon all of us.

The rain has drubbed us in his cold laundry,
The sun has parched us blacker than a crow,
And kites have made each eye a cavity
And torn out beards and eyebrows even so.
There is no resting place where we may go,
But here or there, just as the wind may blow,
We dangle at his pleasure to and fro,
Pocked more by birds than thimble surfaces.
Be not therefore of our fraternity,
But pray God's mercy upon all of us.

Prince Jesus, who hath all in mastery,
Over us let not Hell gain sovereignty,
For of it we are no way curious.
Brothers, see nothing here for mockery,
But pray God's mercy upon all of us.

[ROBERT FITZGERALD]

Lament of the Lovely Helmet-dealer

It seems that I hear that beauty who
Once ran a helmet shop lament
And wish that she were a girl anew,
And utter thus her discontent:
"Thieving old age, malevolent,
Why so soon have you struck me low?
Who cares a damn, who would prevent
My killing myself with one quick blow?

"You've snatched away the sovereignty
That beauty of yore to me consigned
Over churchmen, clerks and merchantry;
For then, no man was born, save blind,
Who wouldn't give all his goods combined,
Though he might have remorse when done,
If unto him I only resigned
What filthy tramps today would shun.

"That thing to many did I deny,
Which wasn't good sense in me, I guess;
I did it for love of a rascally guy,
On whom I bestowed its great largess.
Though many I tricked with wiliness,
By God, I loved him, that wicked lad!
Well, he gave only blows and distress,
And loved me just for the cash I had.

"Though he beat me, kicked me outdoors,
Trampled me down, I loved him still;
Though he broke my back with heavy chores,
If he said come kiss him to my fill,
At once I forgot all hurts and ill.
The gluttonous pimp, vice-ridden, then
Would cuddle me. . . . Much that put in the till!
And what have I got? Shame and sin.

"And now he's dead, thirty years ago,
And I'm still here, a hoary old bum.
When I think of the good times I did know,
What then I was, and what I've become,
When I see my naked shape, all numb
And so completely changed with age,
A meatless, dried-up, shrivelled plum,
I almost lose my mind with rage.

"Where has that smooth forehead gone,
The arching eyebrows, golden hair,
The wide-spaced eyes, that look whereon
I laid for the wisest men a snare,
The straight nose, not too thick nor spare,
Those little ears set well in line,
The dimpled chin, complexion fair,
And those lovely ruby lips of mine?

"Those handsome shoulders, where are they?
Those shapely arms, slim hands likewise,
The small tight breasts, plump hips for play,
Set high, well-made, the proper size
For the jousts of love to utilize,
And those broad loins, that nice plaything
Ensconsed between firm heavy thighs
Within its little garden ring?

"The forehead is wrinkled, gray the hair,
The eyebrows bald, the eyes now blear
That laughed and looked so devil-may-care
They captured all who passed too near;
Nose crooked, its beauty far from here,
Ears sagging, with hairy mosses grown,
Face lifeless, pallid, mottled, drear,
Chin puckered up, lips rough as stone.

"All human beauty finishes thus:
Arms shrunk to bone, hands gnarled and thin,
And shoulders humped and ludicrous;
My bosom? *That?* A flabby hasbeen,
And hips just like the teats—done in.
That plaything? Ugh! And as to thighs,
Not thighs at all, but bags of skin,
Like sausage bladders specked by flies.

"And so our good old days we mourn,
Poor foolish hags, with snivellings,
Huddled on our haunches, forlorn,
In a heap like balls of rags and strings,
By a tiny straw-fire's flickerings,
So soon a-kindle, soon burned out;
And we were once such darling things. . . .
For many, thus will it come about."

[HUBERT CREEKMORE]

Portuguese (Galician)

*The medieval poetry of Portugal is hardly known to any who cannot
read the original texts. The reasons for this are that the texts were
ignored during the Renaissance, then completely lost until their discovery
in the Vatican Library in the late nineteenth century; and since then
almost no translations, except those offered below, have been made.
The poems—about 2000 by some 160 poets—are included in three
Cancioneiros (Song-books) and not only are unlike any other lyrics of
the period, but are probably more indigenous than any save those of
Ireland and Wales.*

*The visiting Troubadours of Provence influenced the work of the
Court poets (see the "Cantiga de Amor" by King Dinis), but the truly
vital literature was the songs—popular songs, in fact, because they
were written and sung by noble and commoner alike. The earliest
existant specimen is by King Sancho I, and the later poets were en-
couraged and patronized by King Dinis, whose grandfather Alfonso X
of Castile had chosen Galician as the language for his Cantigas de
Santa Maria. In this connection it might be said that the theory, not*

wholly tenable, has been advanced that Hispanic poets chose Castilian for epics (such as El Cantar de Mío Cid) *and Galician for lyrics.*

These songs have a static quality, emphasized by their parallelistic structure, as if of oriental languor and melancholy, which may be a residue of the long occupation by the Moors, and certainly stems from origins in Biblical hymns and psalms. Though progression of thought is scarcely perceptible, the songs are full of charm, freshness and grace. All were sung, and much of the music is preserved. Since they were part songs or round songs, a refrain is usual.

The cossante *is a sort of parent form, and its interlocking repetitions can be observed in the translations. Among other types are the dance songs* (bailadas), *dawn songs* (alvoradas), *boat songs* (barcarolas) *and the* cantiga de amigo, *which a girl sings to or about her lover. The* cantiga de amor *was the man's song of his lady, and was of Provençal inspiration. A certain amount of symbolism, suggesting ceremonies and customs of folk culture, will be apparent.*

The lines do not always exactly rhyme in our understanding of the term, nor were they meant to. A rhyme to the Peninsular poets is a matter of vowels, regardless of consonants, but the more cultivated Court poetry rhymes intentionally with all the letters concerned. In the cossante, *a distich with rhyming vowels, feminine ending in* i *and* o, *alternates with a second one in* a *and* o. *For instance, the first two couplets of the "Cossante" of King Dinis end with* pino-amigo *and* ramo-amado, *and the pattern continues throughout.*

Little is known of most of these poets beyond their names. After the death of King Dinis, the singers fell silent for lack of a patron. The singers of native song, that is; for a certain amount of pallid court poetry was still being written. With the opening of the sixteenth century, however, a new and for Portugal almost unique writer emerged: a dramatist, Gil Vincente. The spirit of the people was stirred by discoveries and conquests in America, Africa and Asia, and their pride surged high. Vincente, catching this temper, introduced songs of the people, adapted to his medium, into his plays. Like many poets of the Middle Ages, he wrote in two languages. Ten of his plays are in Castilian, seventeen in Portuguese and fifteen are a mixture of both. The songs below, which are almost the last breath of the indigenous poems, are from his plays.

JOAN ZORRO (*fl.* 1250)

Barcarola

Along by the sea and the river
as a sweetheart will I go,
where the king is arming a vessel,
oh lover, with you I'll go.

Along by the sea and the channel
as a sweetheart will I go,
where the king is arming a galley,
oh lover, with you I'll go.

Where the king is arming a vessel
as a sweetheart will I go,
to carry my virgin riches,
oh lover, with you I'll go.

Where the king is arming a galley,
as a sweetheart will I go,
a boon of riches to carry,
oh lover, with you I'll go.

[SETH G. THORNTON]

MARTIN CODAX (*fl.* 1250)

Cantiga de Amigo

When you know you love a sweetheart,
come straight with me to the sea of Vigo
and we'll bathe ourselves in the waves.

When you know you love a lover,
come straight with me where the sea is tossing
and we'll bathe ourselves in the waves.

Come straight with me to the sea of Vigo,
and there we will see my sweetheart,
and we'll bathe ourselves in the waves.

Come straight with me where the sea is tossing,
and there we will see my lover,
and we'll bathe ourselves in the waves.

[SETH G. THORNTON]

NUNO FERNANDES TORNEOL (13th century)

Alvorada

Arise, friend sleeping in the dawn so chilly:
all the birds in the world of love are chirping,
gaily I'm going.

Arise, friend sleeping in the chill of the morning:
all the birds in the world are singing of loving,
gaily I'm going.

All the birds in the world of love are chirping:
of my love and yours they keep on conversing,
gaily I'm going.

All the birds in the world are singing of loving:
of my love and yours they are speaking together,
gaily I'm going.

Of my love and yours they keep on conversing:
you took down the branches on which they were perching,
gaily I'm going.

Of my love and yours they are speaking together:
you took down the branches on which they were resting,
gaily I'm going.

You took down the branches on which they were perching,
and dried up the springs where they drank when thirsty,
gaily I'm going.

You took down the branches on which they were resting,
and dried up the springs where they bathed in pleasure,
gaily I'm going.

[SETH G. THORNTON]

PERO MEOGO (*fl.* 1250)

Cantiga de Amigo

On the greening grasses
I saw the young does passing,
oh my lover!

On the greening meadows
I saw the wild stags treading,
oh my lover!

And for the pleasure to them,
I washed their horns just budding,
oh my lover!

And to give them pleasure,
I washed my own long tresses,
oh my lover!

Then when I had washed theirs,
with golden cord I laced them,
oh my lover!

Then when I had washed mine,
with golden cord I tied it,
oh my lover!

With golden cord I laced them,
and then for you I waited,
oh my lover!

With golden cord I tied it,
and waited for your coming,
oh my lover!

[SETH G. THORNTON]

Cossante

Tell me, daughter, my lovely daughter,
why did you tarry at the cooling fountain?
Alas, oh lovers!

Tell me, daughter, oh daughter my fairest,
why did you tarry by the fountain's coolness?
Alas, oh lovers!

I tarried, my mother, at the cooling fountain,
the deer from the mountain were splashing the water.
Alas, oh lovers!

I tarried, my mother, by the fountain's coolness,
the deer from the mountain were clouding the runnel.
Alas, oh lovers!

Those are lies, my daughter, lies for your lover,
I never saw stag that would muddle the brooklet.
Alas, oh lovers!

Those are lies, my daughter, lies for your sweetheart,
I never saw stag that would muddle the water.
Alas, oh lovers!

[SETH G. THORNTON]

ROY FERNANDEZ (13th century)

Barcarola

Whenever I see waves surging
and the highest shores receding,
then on me come waves surging
in my heart for the girl so pleasing:
accursèd be the sea
that does such wrong to me!

I never see waves surging
or the highest rocky ledges,
but on me come waves surging
in my heart for the maid so pretty:
accursèd be the sea
that does such wrong to me!

And if I see waves surging
and see the coast line fading,
then on me come waves surging
in my heart for the comely maiden:
accursèd be the sea
that does such wrong to me!

[SETH G. THORNTON]

AIRAS NUNEZ (13th century)

Bailada

Let's dance now, all of us, all of us, oh my maidens,
under these little trees of flowering hazel,
and any girl who is fair as us fair ladies,
if loving a friend perchance,
under these little trees of flowering hazel,
will come to the dance!

Let's dance now, all of us, all of us, oh companions,
under the hazel thicket's spreading branches,
and any girl who's handsome as we are handsome,
if loving a friend perchance,
under the hazel thicket's spreading branches,
will come to the dance!

By God, oh maidens, while we have the time to do it,
under these flowered sprays, let's dance in beauty,
and she who looks as fair as we are looking,
if loving a friend perchance,
under these branches where we dance in blossoms,
will come to the dance!

[SETH G. THORNTON]

KING ALFONSO X (1221–1284)

Cantiga de Santa Maria

Hail Saint Mary!
He who is guided by you
the right must ever do
and flee all folly and sin.

Of a lovely miracle I'll tell the story—
a work of the Mother of the King of glory—
and when you hear it you will not be sorry,
and give me pleasure therein.
Hail Saint Mary!

It was done for a girl young and vivacious,
whose name was Musa, and most fair and gracious
she was and very genteel, but yet flirtatious
and silly had ever been.
Hail Saint Mary!

To do this work, the glorious Virgin Mary
in dreams appeared in splendor legendary,
with many girls of quite extraordinary
beauty; and that was when
(Hail Saint Mary!)

young Musa asked to go with her ere waking;
but said the Saint: If you wish this undertaking,
I beg you, give up mirth and merrymaking,
pride and insolence.
(Hail Saint Mary!)

And if you do, when thirty days are ended,
you'll be with me in this cortege befriended
by these young ladies, who are not foolish-minded—
that fits not discipline.
Hail Saint Mary!

So pleased was Musa with the maids reflected
in dreams, that her bad manners she rejected
and their ways, mild and opposite, she elected,
and longed for nothing again.
Hail Saint Mary!

Her parents, when they saw this alteration,
to Musa spoke, and when they heard her relation
of visions, they begged mercy and dispensation
of her who guards all men.
Hail Saint Mary!

In six and twenty days so dire a fever
on Musa seized that she lay stretched a-shiver;
the Virgin came, and Musa could perceive her,
and said to her: Come then,
(Hail Saint Mary!)

come then for me at once. She said: With pleasure.
And when the term of days their final measure
had run, God lifted up her soul, great treasure,
where live with those akin
(Hail Saint Mary!)

his saints. So may she be our witness-bearer
to plead before the court of wrath and terror,
that it will judge us without sin and error,
to which we say: Amen.

Hail Saint Mary!
He who is guided by you
the right must ever do
and flee all folly and sin.

[SETH G. THORNTON]

KING DINIS (1261–1325)

Cossante

Oh flowers, oh flowers of the tall green pine-tree,
would that you had some news of my sweetheart!
Oh God, and where is he?

Oh flowers, oh flowers of the high green branches,
would that you had some news of my lover!
Oh God, and where is he?

Do you have any news for me of my sweetheart,
who lied when he lay in my embraces?
Oh God, and where is he?

Do you have any news for me of my lover,
who lied to me when he swore his devotion?
Oh God, and where is he?

You ask of me now about your sweetheart,
and I tell you true that he's well and living.
Oh God, and where is he?

You ask me now about your lover,
and I tell you true he's alive and healthy.
Oh God, and where is he?

And I tell you true that he's well and living,
and will be with you at the time appointed.
Oh God, and where is he?

And I tell you true he's alive and healthy,
and will be with you ere the term is ended.
Oh God, and where is he?

[SETH G. THORNTON]

Cantiga de Amor

Fair lady, I see you do complain
because I love you, and in my heart
I grieve, so God forgive my part,
because I see it gives you pain,
and I would gladly loose this chain,
but I can not compel my heart.

For it compelled my mind and wit,
since it threw me in your power,
and for the grief you bear each hour,
by God, lady, I grieve in it,
and I would break from you and quit,
but my heart has reft me of my power.

It forced me, lady, with love so true
that neither strength nor sense have I,
and for the grief you know thereby,
I could not grieve more than I do;
I would wish to bear no love for you,
but still my heart is stronger than I.

[SETH G. THORNTON]

Alvorada

The girl arose so lovely,
arose at dawning,
and went to wash her blouses
by the brookside,
she went to wash at dawning.

The girl arose so pretty,
arose at dawning,
and went to wash chemises
by the brookside,
she went to wash at dawning.

And went to wash her blouses,
arose at dawning,
the wind then shifted courses,
by the brookside,
she went to wash at dawning.

And went to wash chemises,
arose at dawning,
away the wind blew them freely,
by the brookside,
she went to wash at dawning.

The wind then shifted courses,
arose at dawning,
it put the girl in a temper,
by the brookside,
she went to wash at dawning.

Away the wind blew them freely,
arose at dawning,
it made the fair girl angry,
by the brookside,
she went to wash at dawning.

[SETH G. THORNTON]

GIL VINCENTE (c. 1470–c. 1540)

Cantiga

Take away from me my eyes,
my life, my serenity,
for you love me, that I see.
Your own eyes, lady of mine,
lady of beauty sans peer,
with every moment of time
yield the woe of a thousand years.
I'll have no luck, I fear.
Dearest, you don't look at me,
for you love me, that I see.

[SETH G. THORNTON]

Esparsa

The longing a wife must bear
kills the heart and the soul,
for time doesn't lessen at all
the torment lingering there.
And you, if you go from me,
on other beauties will gaze,
speak and you hear a sweet phrase;
but without you I do not see,
save the darkest things always.

[SETH G. THORNTON]

Spanish (Castilian)

*T*he earliest lyrics, before 1040, were Mozarabic—love songs composed in rudimentary Spanish with a sprinkling of Hebrew and Arabic.
Sung in territory occupied by the Moors, they were much like the
parallelistic songs of Portugal. In fact, the first popular lyrics eschewing
the polyglot style were written in Galician, or drew on its songs for
inspiration. But for some time many Spanish authors chose to write
lyrics in the northern Portuguese dialect.

By the time the first known poet had appeared, lyric models of
neighboring Provence and France were already being imitated. Troubadours and Trouvères were indeed everywhere, but they, along with many
other creative and influential persons, were especially in Spain. They
followed in the train of warriors crusading against the Moorish conquest,
they sought patrons in the Spanish courts. One who needed no patron,
the French Count Thibaut of Champagne, became King of Navarre
in 1234 by succession—an instance of the close contact through dynastic
marriages of Spanish kingdoms and Franco-Provençal kingdoms. To
complete the invasion of foreign cultures, there was a constant

pilgrimage from all lands to the shrine of Santiago at Compostela.

For the most part, Spanish poetry at this time was written in cuaderna via, *quatrains of alexandrine lines all in the same rhyme—and of vast monotony. The form was still used by the first poet of any great interest, Juan Ruiz, Archpriest of Hita and a worldly amorous man for all his clerical cloth. However, he managed to loosen up the* cuaderna via *and to insert into his* Libro de buen amor, *a miscellany of his adventures and poems, a few samples of popular song. The book, which bears slight resemblances to Chaucer's* Canterbury Tales, *gives a faithful, surprisingly realistic but sardonic view of Ruiz' world. "Mountain Song" is in some ways a parody of the courtly pastorela, and strikes a note similar to Guillem IX's "Poem" in the Provençal section.*

Few of the other poets are included in this group, since they imitate work already represented elsewhere in its primal state. The space they might fill is given to anonymous songs and romances. The songs show some kinship with the songs of Portugal, and in some specimens not offered here are virtually identical in structure and tone. The romances, counterparts of the ballad but with a distinctive flavor and structure, seem to spring from lost epics, or be favorite recollected passages from them.

Interest in this native poetry was of benefit to the Marquès de Santillana. In spite of his international culture, including Italian masters, he was able to write a few poems of individual artistry and natural freshness. "Villancico" may be compared in a few traits with the French "Three Sisters."

In the "Coplas" of Jorge Manrique, Spain has its greatest poem of this period and, to some, of the centuries to follow. Though the thought and sentiment are as old as time, as commonplace as air, the poet welded them into a solid impressive form that has a lasting appeal to humanity. The poem has been called "an almost matchless masterpiece" and "one of the lyrical masterpieces of all time."

JUAN RUIZ, ARCHPRIEST OF HITA
(1283–1350)

Mountain Song

One morning as I was traversing
Malangosto Pass at a trot,
as soon as my head showed, with cursing
a mountain girl pounced like a shot.
"You rascal," she said, "where you going?
What you seeking, or think worth knowing
in this narrow mountainous spot?"

I gave her an answer quite civil:
"Sotos-alvos is where I am bound."
She replied: "You'll get the devil
by throwing such wild talk around;
because through the pass in this sector,
where I'm keeper and toll-collector,
goes no man who's sane and sound."

That pigeon-toed, pock-marked creature
blockaded my path like a ram,
saying, "Squire, by heck, you can seat your
self here and stay meek as a lamb,
till you pledge me a fee to delight me;
however you threaten and fight me,
you'll not climb this road, by damn."

I told her: "By Jesus, you cow-girl,
don't hinder my journey today,
get away from the highroad now, girl,
for I've nothing to give you for pay."
She said: "Then turn back, young rover,
by the summit you'll have to cross over,
for you'll get no passage this way."

That devilish pug-nose brawler—
may St. Julian curse her somehow!—
she hooked her sheepcrook at my collar,
and whirled her sling at my brow,
and jabbing a dart at me, grumbled:
"By the Lord who on earth was humbled,
you'll pay the sheep-toll right now."

It was snowing right hard and hailing.
Then Pug-nose let out a great cry,
started making wild threats and railing:
"Pay up, or you'll fight and know why!"
"By God, you gorgeous belle, you,"
I said, "I've something to tell you,
but I'd like a fire to talk by."

"I'll take you up there to my shanty,
and show you the proper highway,
build a fire that won't be scanty,
give you bread and wine if you say.
But golly! just promise a present
and I'll think you're not a peasant.
It will be your lucky day."

From fear and cold all a-shiver,
I promised she'd get some clothes,
for her dress I said I'd give her
a brooch and a locket with bows.
"I'll give you lots more, old fellow!
Come along, this way!"—what a bellow!—
"Don't be scared of the ice! Here goes!"

Then she grabbed my hand and flung me
right up on her shoulders with skill,
like a light hunting pouch she hung me,
and strode up the slope with a will.
"Poor lamb, don't be scared, fiddle-diddle!
I'll give you some real nice victuals,
just the sort we have in the hills."

For shelter she easily brought me
to where her trading hut stood,
and a fire of oak logs she got me,
and some rabbits caught in the wood,
and partridges baked very pretty,
a big loaf of bread that was gritty,
and meat of a kid that was good.

A pint of wine, rather mellow,
and butter from cows she set out,
and plenty of cheese, smoky yellow,
and milk and some cream and a trout;
and said: "Come on, chum, don't worry,
let's eat this dry bread in a hurry,
after that we'll have a nice bout."

When I'd sat there a bit by the embers,
I thawed and my chill was all gone;
As I warmed up my frozen members,
I started to smile and to yawn.
The shepherdess looked at me, smirky,
and "Aha!" she said, "now, you turkey,
I think you're about to catch on!"

That low-minded cow-girl beckoned:
"Let's wrestle a short round—yes?
Get up from there right this second,
take off all those clothes—undress!"
She seized on my wrist, undaunted;
I had to do just what she wanted.
You think I got off cheap, I guess!

[HUBERT CREEKMORE]

Street Song

My eyes will never see the light,
For I have lost the Cross outright.

Dame Cross, my crossroad, wife to the baker,
My love-chum I had thought to make her,
Took a byway for highway—dumb mistaker,
    Like an Andalouse blatherskite.

Thinking to get her, I without heeding
Sent Ramrod Garcia to do my pleading,
To superintend the whole proceeding
    And be my agent and guide.

He said he'd be glad to do the favor,
And became her favorite misbehaver,
Threw me the crust to chew with no flavor,
    And ate bread sweet and white.

He promised to give her, as I directed,
Some choicest wheat that I'd collected,
And the sly deceitful traitor defected,
    And gave her a bunny that night.

God damn a messenger who's such a blunt man,
So quick on the draw, untrusty, a stunt man!
May God not thrive such a bunny-huntsman
    Who goes on the chase to spite!

                              [HUBERT CREEKMORE]

ANONYMOUS ROMANCES
(14th–15th centuries)

Mudarra and Rodrigo

A-hunting went the noble knight,
And Don Rodrigo was he hight,
    Rodrigo, he of Lara;
The noon-day heat was very great.
Beneath a shady beech he sate,
    And cursed the young Mudarra;
"Thou son of Moorish maid," quoth he,
"If I should lay my hands on thee,
Thou bastard of a cursèd race,
I'd tear thy heart from out its place."

Thus spoke the lordling in his pride;
A stranger youth came to his side,
    And due obeisance made;
"Sir knight, God's blessing rest on thee,
Beneath the green and shady tree;"
    The knight he bowed, and said:
"Good squire, thy coming it is blest,
Pray sit thee down a while and rest!"
    "Nay, good sir knight, before I go,
Thine honored name I fain would know."

Then up and spake the knight of fame:
"'Tis Don Rodrigo is my name,
   Rodrigo, I, of Lara;
My sister, Lady Sancha fair,
Wedded Gonzalo, Lara's heir;
My nephews were the youthful band,
Whose fate is known through all the land,
   The seven sons of Lara;
I wait Mudarra in this glade,
Son of the cursèd Moorish maid;
If he were now before my sight,
I'd tear his heart out to the light."

"If thou hast come from Lara's stem,
And Don Rodrigo is thy name,
   Then I'm the young Mudarra,
Born of the Moorish renegade,
Gonzalo's son by Moorish maid;
I am the Lady Sancha's heir,
And these, they were my brothers fair,
   The seven sons of Lara;
Their lives, O traitor, thou didst sell,
In dark Arabiana's dell,
May God above be in my aid,
And I will lay thee with the dead!"

"Wait here a space within this field,
Till I shall bring my sword and shield,
   I'll fight with thee, Mudarra!"
"The space thou gavest them, I'll give,
One moment more thou hast to live,
Go, traitor, to thy doom below,
My father's curse and Sancha's foe!"
   Struck home the young Mudarra.

[JAMES Y. GIBSON]

The Moorish King Who Lost Alhama

The Moorish King rides up and down,
Through Granada's royal town;
From Elvira's gates to those
Of Bivarambla on he goes.
     Woe is me, Alhama!

Letters to the monarch tell
How Alhama's city fell;
In the fire the scroll he threw,
And the messenger he slew.
     Woe is me, Alhama!

He quits his mule and mounts his horse
And through the street directs his course;
Through the street of Zacatín
To the Alhambra spurring in.
     Woe is me, Alhama!

When the Alhambra's walls he gained,
On the moment he ordained
That the trumpet straight should sound
With the silver clarion round.
     Woe is me, Alhama!

And when the hollow drums of war
Beat the loud alarm afar,
That the Moors of town and plain
Might answer to the martial strain,
     Woe is me, Alhama!

Then the Moors, by this aware
That bloody Mars recalled them there,
One by one, and two by two,
To a mighty squadron grew.
     Woe is me, Alhama!

Out then spoke an agèd Moor
In these words, the King before,
"Wherefore call on us, O King?
What may mean this gathering?"
               Woe is me, Alhama!

"Friends, ye have, alas, to know
Of a most disastrous blow;
That the Christians, stern and bold,
Have obtained Alhama's hold."
               Woe is me, Alhama!

Out then spoke old Alfaquí,
With his beard so white to see,
"Good King! thou art justly served!
Good King! this thou hast deserved!
               Woe is me, Alhama!

"By thee were slain, in evil hour,
The Abencerrage, Granada's flower;
And strangers were received by thee
Of Cordova the chivalry.
               Woe is me, Alhama!

"And for this, O King, is sent
On thee a double chastisement;
Thee and thine, thy crown and realm,
One last wreck shall overwhelm.
               Woe is me, Alhama!"
                    [LORD BYRON]

Montesinos and Durandarte

Closed in death lies Durandarte,
   Montesinos sees him die
And, awhile in sorrow musing
   Heaves a deep distressing sigh.

When he saw him mute and lifeless,
   And the warmth his corse forsook,
From his friend his sword and helmet
   And his armour off he took.

Then with bitter anguish weeping,
   He fulfils his last request;
And, the hero's left side opening,
   Takes the heart out of his breast.

When he saw it lie before him
   Loud he raised the voice of woe:—
"Cousin, like a fountain streaming
   "O'er thy heart my tears shall flow.

"Never France a warrior boasted
   "More undaunted in the fight:
"Mild in peace, in war a lion:
   "Never liv'd a better knight.

"To the grave thy corse consigning,
   "Long thy virtues still shall live;
"But thy heart to fair Belerma
   "Will I, as thou bad'st me, give."

Deep he digs the grave, the body
   Leaving to its native clay;
Takes a parting look, and, weeping,
   Bears the hero's heart away:

From all eyes his face concealing
   Till he had Belerma seen;
Round his head his helmet fastening,
   On he rides with pensive mien;

And, the gates of Paris entering,
   To Belerma's palace goes,
To distract her gentle bosom,
   And afflict her soul with woes.

           [THOMAS RODD]

Count Arnaldos

Whoever could have had such fortune
   On the waters of the sea,
As came unto the Count Arnaldos
   The morn of Saint John's day!
With falcon sitting on his gauntlet,
   He'd gone to hunt for game,
When he espied a ship approaching,
   Trying to make the shore.
Its sails all of silk were fashioned,
   Its shrouds of gossamer gold,
And the sailor at the galley's tiller
   Was singing a song as he came,
That made the waves lie smooth and placid,
   And winds sink down to a lull,
And fish that swim in the dark abysses
   It made to swim to the top,
And the birds that overhead were flying
   It made to perch on the mast.

Then up and spoke the Count Arnaldos,
    Plain shall you hear his words:
"For God's sake, I do beg you, Sailor,
    Now teach to me this song."
To him the sailor made his answer,
    This answer then gave he:
"I teach this song of mine to no one
    But him who comes with me."

                        [RICHARD BEAUMONT]

ANONYMOUS

Two Songs

Moon, moon shining bright,
All night long you shed your light.

Oh moon, moon shining bright,
White and silvered over,
All night long you shed your light
On my pretty girl, my beloved.
Sweetheart, shining bright,
All night long you shed your light.

      *   *   *

All are asleep, heart so true,
All are asleep—but not you!

The grief that you've discovered
Always keeps you wakeful,
For the heart that's hurt will suffer,
Remembering love it knew.
All are asleep, heart so true,
All are asleep—but not you!

                        [RICHARD BEAUMONT]

Four Songs

These pains of mine, oh mother,
Of love, of love, are born.

Come, come out, my lady,
From under the orange trees.
You're so lovely and fair
That you'll be burned by the air
Of love—oh yes indeed!

*   *   *

If the night's so full of darkness
And so short the road between,
Why don't you come, dear friend?

Midnight has passed and gone
And he comes not who makes me suffer:
My bad luck makes him stay away.
How unlucky was I born!
He keeps me living in anguish
And seems to be my enemy.
Why don't you come, dear friend?

*   *   *

Unhappily married beauty,
Of all the fair girls I knew,
Remember how much, how deeply,
Lady, I once loved you.

Resplendant star of the dawn,
Shadow of all my pleasure,
Of women the crown and treasure,
The glory of this our time;
Supreme, most excellent one
Above all I ever knew,
Remember how much, how deeply,
Lady, I once loved you.

*   *   *

Under the oak tree, oak tree,
Under the oak tree.

I was going, dear mother,
On a pilgrimage bent.
To walk in more devotion,
Without companions I went,
Under the oak tree.

To walk in more devotion,
Without companions I went;
I left the road I had followed
And took one quite different,
Under the oak tree.

I found I was lost completely
On a mountain unknown,
And lay myself down to sleep
At the foot of the oak alone,
Under the oak tree.

In the middle of the night
I woke, a little distressed,
And found myself in the arms
Of the man I love the best,
Under the oak tree.

I was sad, poor maiden,
When day broke on my rest,
For I was truly enjoying
The man that I love the best,
Under the oak tree.

May it then be most blest,
Such pilgrimage and quest,
Under the oak tree.

[SETH G. THORNTON]

MARQUÉS DE SANTILLANA (1398–1458)

Villancico For His Three Daughters

In a park, delightful and fair
with flowers and roses around,
three beautiful ladies I found,
all wishing for love to be there.
With lively goodwill to share,
I went forth to greet them then;
and one of them did begin
to sing this decorous air:
    "They all are waiting for me;
    such guards I never did see."

To gaze on the grace that crowned
these loveliest ladies yet seen,
I hid behind branches of green
and sat on the grassy ground.
The second with sadness profound
began soft sighing ere long
and singing this little song
with purest control and sound:
    "The girl with a love of her own—
    how shall she sleep all alone?"

To keep from causing alarm,
I wouldn't go nearer the three
who with good method and charm
were singing harmoniously.
The last, with fair face to see,
said: "Ladies so high-born and young,
since both in your turn have sung,
the turn has come now to me:
    'Let the rogue bear torments grim;
    may God avenge me on him'."

And after they'd sung so sweet,
these ladies I thus commend,
I sadly came from my retreat
like a shelterless man, chagrinned.
They said to me then: "Dear friend,
the one that we seek is not you,
but sing, since we're singing too:
    'Sighing the girl passed by,
    but not for me were her sighs,
    as I well could realize'."

                [RICHARD BEAUMONT]

JORGE MANRIQUE (1440–1479)

Coplas on the Death of His Father

O, let the soul her slumbers break!
Let thought be quickened and awake,—
    Awake to see
How soon this life is past and gone,
And death comes softly stealing on,—
    How silently!
Swiftly our pleasures glide away:
Our hearts recall the distant day
    With many sighs;
The moments that are speeding fast
We heed not; but the past—the past—
    More highly prize.

Onward its course the present keeps,
Onward the constant current sweeps,
　　Till life is done;
And did we judge of time aright,
The past and future in their flight
　　Would be as one.
Let no one fondly dream again
That Hope and all her shadowy train
　　Will not decay;
Fleeting as were the dreams of old,
Remembered like a tale that's told,
　　They pass away.

Our lives are rivers gliding free
To that unfathomed, boundless sea,
　　The silent grave:
Thither all earthly pomp and boast
Roll to be swallowed up and lost
　　In one dark wave.
Thither the mighty torrents stray,
Thither the brook pursues its way,
　　And tinkling rill.
There all are equal. Side by side,
The poor man and the son of pride
　　Lie calm and still.

I will not here invoke the throng
Of orators and sons of song,
　　The deathless few;
Fiction entices and deceives,
And sprinkling o'er her fragrant leaves
　　Lies poisonous dew.
To One alone my thoughts arise,—
The Eternal Truth,—the Good and Wise:
　　To Him I cry,
Who shared on earth our common lot,
But the world comprehended not
　　His deity.

This world is but the rugged road
Which leads us to the bright abode
    Of peace above;
So let us choose that narrow way
Which leads no traveller's foot astray
    From realms of love.
Our cradle is the starting-place;
In life we run the onward race,
    And reach the goal;
When, in the mansions of the blest,
Death leaves to its eternal rest
    The weary soul.

Did we but use it as we ought,
This world would school each wandering thought
    To its high state.
Faith wings the soul beyond the sky,
Up to the better world on high
    For which we wait.
Yes,—the glad messenger of love,
To guide us to our home above,
    The Saviour came;
Born amid mortal cares and fears,
He suffered in this vale of tears
    A death of shame.

Behold of what delusive worth
The bubbles we pursue on earth,
    The shapes we chase,
Amid a world of treachery!
They vanish ere death shuts the eye,
    And leave no trace.
Time steals them from us,—chances strange,
Disastrous accidents, and change,
    That come to all:
Even in the most exalted state,
Relentless sweeps the stroke of fate;
    The strongest fall.

Tell me,—the charms that lovers seek
In the clear eye and blushing cheek,—
    The hues that play
O'er rosy lips and brow of snow,—
When hoary age approaches slow,
    Ah, where are they?
The cunning skill, the curious arts,
The glorious strength that youth imparts
    In life's first stage—
These shall become a heavy weight,
When Time swings wide his outward gate
    To weary age.

The noble blood of Gothic name,
Heroes emblazoned high to fame
    In long array,—
How, in the onward course of time,
The landmarks of that race sublime
    Were swept away!
Some, the degraded slaves of lust,
Prostrate and trampled in the dust,
    Shall rise no more;
Others by guilt and crime maintain
The scutcheon that without a stain
    Their fathers bore.

Wealth and the high estate of pride,
With what untimely speed they glide,
    How soon depart!
Bid not the shadowy phantoms stay,—
The vassals of a mistress they,
    Of fickle heart.
These gifts in Fortune's hands are found;
Her swift-revolving wheel turns round,
    And they are gone!
No rest the inconstant goddess knows,
But changing, and without repose,
    Still hurries on.

Even could the hand of avarice save
Its gilded baubles, till the grave
    Reclaimed its prey,
Let none on such poor hopes rely;
Life, like an empty dream flits by,
    And where are they?
Earthly desires and sensual lust
Are passions springing from the dust,—
    They fade and die;
But, in the life beyond the tomb,
They seal the immortal spirit's doom
    Eternally!

The pleasures and delights which mask
In treacherous smiles life's serious task,
    What are they all,
But the fleet coursers of the chase,—
And death an ambush in the race,
    Wherein we fall?
No foe, no dangerous pass we heed,
Brook no delay,—but onward speed,
    With loosened rein;
And when the fatal snare is near,
We strive to check our mad career,
    But strive in vain.

Could we new charms to age impart,
And fashion with a cunning art
    The human face,
As we can clothe the soul with light,
And make the glorious spirit bright
    With heavenly grace,—
How busily, each passing hour,
Should we exert that magic power!
    What ardor show
To deck the sensual slave of sin.
Yet leave the freeborn soul within
    In weeds of woe!

Monarchs, the powerful and the strong,
Famous in history and in song
  Of olden time,
Saw, by the stern decrees of fate,
Their kingdoms lost, and desolate
  Their race sublime.
Who is the champion? Who the strong?
Pontiff and priest, and sceptered throng?
  On these shall fall
As heavily the hand of Death,
As when it stays the shepherd's breath
  Beside his stall.

I speak not of the Trojan name,—
Neither its glory nor its shame
  Has met our eyes;
Nor of Rome's great and glorious dead,—
Though we have heard so oft, and read,
  Their histories.
Little avails it now to know
Of ages past so long ago,
  Nor how they rolled;
Our theme shall be of yesterday
Which to oblivion sweeps away,
  Like days of old.

Where is the king Don Juan? Where
Each royal prince and noble heir
  Of Aragon?
Where are the courtly gallantries?
The deeds of love and high emprise,
  In battle done?
Tourney and joust, that charmed the eye,
And scarf, and gorgeous panoply,
  And nodding plume,—
What are they but a pageant scene?
What but the garlands, gay and green
  That deck the tomb?

Where are the high-born dames, and where
Their gay attire and jewelled hair,
    And odors sweet?
Where are the gentle knights, that came
To kneel, and breathe love's ardent flame,
    Low at their feet?
Where is the song of Troubadour?
Where are the lute and gay tambour
    They loved of yore?
Where is the mazy dance of old,—
The flowering robes, inwrought with gold,
    The dancers wore?

And he who next the sceptre swayed,
Henry, whose royal court displayed
    Such power and pride,—
O, in what winning smiles arrayed,
The world its various pleasures laid
    His throne beside!
But, O, how false and full of guile
That world, which wore so soft a smile
    But to betray!
She, that had been his friend before,
Now from the fated monarch tore
    Her charms away.

The countless gifts,—the stately walls,
The royal palaces, and halls
    All filled with gold;
Plate with armorial bearings wrought,
Chambers with ample treasures fraught
    Of wealth untold;
The noble steeds, and harness bright,
The gallant lord, and stalwart knight,
    In rich array;—
Where shall we seek them now? Alas
Like the bright dew-drops on the grass,
    They passed away.

His brother, too, whose factious zea
Usurped the sceptre of Castille,
   Unskilled to reign,—
What a gay, brilliant court had he,
When all the flower of chivalry
   Was in his train!
But he was mortal, and the breath
That flamed from the hot forge of Death
   Blasted his years;
Judgment of God! that flame by thee,
When raging fierce and fearfully,
   Was quenched in tears!

Spain's haughty Constable,—the true
And gallant Master,—whom we knew
   Most loved of all,—
Breathe not a whisper of his pride;
He on the gloomy scaffold died,—
   Ignoble fall!
The countless treasures of his care,
His hamlets green and cities fair,
   His mighty power,—
What were they all but grief and shame,
Tears and a broken heart, when came
   The parting hour?

His other brothers, proud and high,—
Masters, who, in prosperity,
   Might rival kings,—
Who made the bravest and the best
The bondsmen of their high behest,
   Their underlings,—
What was their prosperous estate,
When high exalted and elate
   With power and pride?
What, but a transient gleam of light,—
A flame, which, glaring at its height,
   Grew dim and died?

So many a duke of royal name,
Marquis and count of spotless fame,
    And baron brave,
That might the sword of empire wield,—
All these, O Death, hast thou concealed
    In the dark grave!
Their deeds of mercy and of arms,
In peaceful days, or war's alarms,
    When thou dost show,
O Death, thy stern and angry face,
One stroke of thy all-powerful mace
    Can overthrow!

Unnumbered hosts, that threaten nigh,—
Pennon and standard flaunting high,
    And flag displayed,—
High battlements intrenched around,
Bastion, and moated wall, and mound,
    And palisade,
And covered trench, secure and deep,—
All these cannot one victim keep,
    O Death, from thee,
When thou dost battle in thy wrath,
And thy strong shafts pursue their path
    Unerringly!

O world! so few the years we live,
Would that the life which thou dost give
    Were life indeed!
Alas! thy sorrows fall so fast,
Our happiest hour is when, at last,
    The soul is freed.
Our days are covered o'er with grief,
And sorrows neither few nor brief
    Veil all in gloom;
Left desolate of real good,
Within this cheerless solitude
    No pleasures bloom.

Thy pilgrimage begins in tears,
And ends in bitter doubts and fears,
 Or dark despair;
Midway so many toils appear,
That he who lingers longest here
 Knows most of care.
Thy goods are bought with many a groan,
By the hot sweat of toil alone,
 And weary hearts;
Fleet-footed is the approach of woe,
But with a lingering step and slow
 Its form departs.

And he, the good man's shield and shade,
To whom all hearts their homage paid,
 As Virtue's son—
Rodrick Manrique,—he whose name
Is written on the scroll of Fame,
 Spain's champion;
His signal deeds and prowess high
Demand no pompous eulogy,—
 Ye saw his deeds!
Why should their praise in verse be sung?
The name that dwells on every tongue
 No minstrel needs.

To friends a friend;—how kind to all
The vassals of this ancient hall
 And feudal fief!
To foes how stern a foe was he!
And to the valiant and the free
 How brave a chief!
What prudence with the old and wise!
What grace in youthful gaieties!
 In all how sage!
Benignant to the serf and slave,
He showed the base and falsely brave
 A lion's rage.

His was Octavian's prosperous star,
The rush of Caesar's conquering car
 At battle's call;
His, Scripio's virtue; his, the skill
And the indomitable will
 Of Hannibal.
His was a Trajan's goodness; his
A Titus' noble charities
 And righteous laws;
The arm of Hector, and the might
Of Tully, to maintain the right
 In truth's just cause;

The clemency of Antonine;
Aurelius' countenance divine,
 Firm, gentle, still;
The eloquence of Adrian;
And Theodosius' love to man,
 And generous will;
In tented field and bloody fray,
An Alexander's vigorous sway
 And stern command;
The faith of Constantine; ay, more,—
The fervent love Camillus bore
 His native land.

He left no well filled treasury,
He heaped no pile of riches high,
 Nor massive plate;
He fought the Moors,—and, in their fall,
City and tower and castled wall
 Were his estate.
Upon the hard-fought battle-ground
Brave steeds and gallant riders found
 A common grave;
And there the warriors' hand did gain
The rents, and the long vassal train,
 That conquest gave.

And if, of old, his halls displayed
The honored and exalted grade
     His worth had gained,
So, in the dark, disastrous hour,
Brothers and bondsmen of his power
     His hand sustained.
After high deeds, not left untold,
In the stern warfare which of old
     'Twas his to share,
Such noble leagues he made, that more
And fairer regions than before
     His guerdon were.

These are the records, half effaced,
Which with the hand of youth, he traced
     On history's page;
But with fresh victories he drew
Each fading character anew
     In his old age.
By his unrivalled skill, by great
And veteran service to the state,
     By worth adored,
He stood, in his high dignity,
The proudest knight of chivalry,—
     Knight of the Sword.

He found his cities and domains
Beneath a tyrant's galling chains
     And cruel power;
But, by fierce battle and blockade,
Soon his own banner was displayed
     From every tower.
By the tried valor of his hand
His monarch and his native land
     Were nobly served;—
Let Portugal repeat the story,
And proud Castille, who shared the glory
     His arms deserved.

And when so oft, for weal or woe,
His life upon the fatal throw
    Had been cast down,—
When he had served, with patriot zeal
Beneath the banner of Castille,
    His sovereign's crown,—
And done such deeds of valor strong,
That neither history nor song
    Can count them all;
Then, on Ocaña's castled rock,
Death at his portal came to knock,
    With sudden call,—

Saying, "Good Cavalier, prepare
To leave this world of toil and care
    With joyful mien;
Let thy strong heart of steel this day
Put on its armour for the fray,—
    The closing scene.
Since thou hast been, in battle-strife,
So prodigal of health and life,
    For earthly fame,
Let virtue nerve thy heart again;
Loud on the last stern battle-plain
    They call thy name.

"Think not the struggle that draws near
Too terrible for man, nor fear
    To meet the foe;
Nor let thy noble spirit grieve,
Its life of glorious fame to leave
    On earth below.
A life of honor and of worth
Has no eternity on earth,—
    'Tis but a name;
And yet its glory far exceeds
That base sensual life which leads
    To want and shame.

"The eternal life, beyond the sky,
Wealth cannot purchase, nor the high
    And proud estate;
The soul in dalliance laid,—the spirit
Corrupt with sin,—shall not inherit
    A joy so great.
But the good monk, in cloistered cell,
Shall gain it by his book and bell,
    His prayers and tears;
And the brave knight, whose arm endures
Fierce battle, and against the Moors
    His standard rears.

"And thou, brave knight, whose hand has poured
The life-blood of the pagan horde
    O'er all the land,
In heaven shalt thou receive, at length,
The guerdon of thy earthly strength
    And dauntless hand.
Cheered onward by this promise sure,
Strong in the faith entire and pure
    Thou dost profess,
Depart,—thy hope is certainty;—
The third—the better life on high
    Thou dost possess."

—"O Death, no more, no more delay!
My spirit longs to flee away
    And be at rest,—
The will of Heaven my will shall be,—
I bow to the divine decree,
    To God's behest.
My soul is ready to depart,—
No thought rebels,—the obedient heart
    Breathes forth no sigh;
The wish on earth to linger still
Were vain, when 'tis God's sovereign will
    That we shall die.

"O thou, that for our sins didst take
A human form, and humbly make
    Thy home on earth!
Thou, that to thy divinity
A human nature didst ally
    By mortal birth,—
And in that form didst suffer here
Torment, and agony, and fear,
    So patiently!
By thy redeeming grace alone,
And not for merits of my own,
    O, pardon me!"

As thus the dying warrior prayed,
Without one gathering mist or shade
    Upon his mind,—
Encircled by his family,
Watched by affection's gentle eye,
    So soft and kind,—
His soul to Him who gave it rose.
God lead it to its long repose,
    Its glorious rest!
And, though the warrior's sun has set,
Its light shall linger round us yet,
    Bright, radiant, blest.

[H. W. LONGFELLOW]

Italian

In the first centuries of the Middle Ages, the purest Latin on the Italian peninsula was spoken in Rome, while a vernacular was used in the provinces as late as the tenth century. This rude, non-classical usage developed into various dialects according to the regions, but eventually emerged as a language (still divided into dialects today) which was called Italian. Because there was little sense of nationality in the people, and the social and economic pattern of government operated against unification, Italian was one of the last of the Romance literatures to appear.

Many authors were of course writing in Latin; others had turned to French and hybrid dialects; still others to the much admired Provençal. Poetry in Italian properly begins with the Sicilian School, a group of poets assembled by Emperor Frederick II at Palermo. Here Jacopo da Lentino may have "invented" the sonnet, working, as all these poets did, from Provençal models and themes.

It was not long, however, before the Sicilian School was supplanted by the Tuscan School, made up mostly of Florentines such as Guinicelli and Cavalcanti, who demanded more delicacy in manner and diction, and fresh grace and refinement of style. Their work was characterized, in fact, as the "dolce stil nuovo"*—the sweet new style—but the form and basic thought were essentially Provençal. They did enlarge and deepen the thematic matter, however, by adding to the chivalric worship of the ideal unattainable woman, many symbolic and metaphoric concepts drawn from philosophy and theology.*

Cino da Pistoia and Dante were younger members of this "school" and passed on the ideals of their art to later poets. Dante's greatest work is, needless to say, the long complex Divine Comedy, *for which he devised the interlocking* terza rima. *In his short poems he followed accepted models, including adaptation of Arnaut Daniel's new sestina form, but they are never negligible poetry and have maintained down the centuries a broad popularity that his masterpiece never won.*

Amid the sweet sounds of the "new style", there was also a type of "realistic" poetry, dealing with plain matters rather than soaring contemplations of love and heaven. Among those who wrote such poems were Cecco Angiolieri, Rustico di Filippo and Folgore da San Geminiano. The earthy quality of unnoble passion and genre description makes them a pleasant relief to the elevated tone of their contemporaries.

Petrarch and Boccaccio followed in the path of Dante and the Tuscan School, but the latter leaned more and more toward a realism which finally found its true expression in his prose Decameron, *though not before he had produced a goodly body of poems and established a new stanzaic form, the* ottava rima. *Petrarch was a highly accomplished poet of love, and his ballades and sonnets have had world-wide influence. To some degree, he abandoned the philosophizing, moralizing tone of his predecessors in favor of a simpler expression of emotion. By translating and imitating his work 150 years later, Sir Thomas Wyatt and the Earl of Surrey wrote the first sonnets in English.*

The two Italian poets figured in the beginnings of Humanism, that rediscovery of ancient classics which fired the imagination of Europe, and they wrote much in Latin—epics, lyrics, prose—and in general helped to break rich ground for later generations. With their deaths shortly before the close of the fourteenth century, they brought to a close the Middle Ages for all of Europe. For at the same time, they had ushered in the Renaissance, which was to spread as fast and far as the early Provençal singers did, and give a new outlook, a fresh questing spirit to man.

JACOPO DA LENTINO (*c.* 1180–*c.* 1240)

Canzonetta

My lady mine, I send
  These sighs in joy to thee;
Though, loving till the end,
  There were no hope for me
That I should speak my love;
  And I have loved indeed,
  Though, having fearful-heed,
It was not spoken of.

Thou art so high and great
  That whom I love I fear;
Which thing to circumstate
  I have no messenger:
Wherefore to Love I pray,
  On whom each lover cries,
  That these my tears and sighs
Find unto thee a way.

Well have I wish'd, when I
  At heart with sighs have ached,
That there were in each sigh
  Spirit and intellect,
The which, where thou dost sit,
  Should kneel and sue for aid,
  Since I am thus afraid
And have no strength for it.

Thou, lady, killest me,
  Yet keepest me in pain,
For thou must surely see
  How, fearing, I am fain.
Ah! why not send me still
  Some solace, small and slight,
  So that I should not quite
Despair of thy good will?

Thy grace, all else above,
  Even now while I implore
Enamoureth my love
  To love thee still the more.
Yet scarce should I know well
  A greater love to gain,
  Even if a greater pain,
Lady, were possible.

Joy did that day relax
  My grief's continual stress,
When I essay'd in wax
  Thy beauty's life-likeness.
Ah! much more beautiful
  Than golden-hair'd Yseult,—
  Who mak'st all men exult,
Who bring'st all women dule.

And certes without blame
  Thy love might fall on me,
Though it should chance my name
  Were never heard of thee.
Yea, for thy love, in fine,
  Lentino gave me birth,
  Who am not nothing worth
If worthy to be thine.

                              [D. G. ROSSETTI]

JACOPONE DA TODI (1230–1306)

Dialogue of the Body with the Soul, which is Leading it to Judgment

—O flesh now putrefied,   I'm spirit in agony;
Rise up immediately,   we're doomed both to be tried.

The angel is trumpeting   in tones dread and severe:
We must before the King   without delay appear;
You lived once arguing   that we need have no fear:
I erred to trust and hear   when you had sin for guide.—

—Then you're my soul I see,   genteel, intelligent!
Since you withdrew from me   again to naught I went;
Keep me now company   that I bear no torment:
I see folk pestilent   with faces evil-eyed.—

—Those are the demons cursed   with whom you now must
                                                        dwell;
You should not ask the worst: what you must suffer well,
My thoughts are too dispersed   to bring myself to tell.
Were seas with ink to swell,   the sum they could not write.—

—I cannot go ahead   for I'm so worn and spent
That I am almost dead,   I feel stern death commence;
From me you would have fled: each joint in me you rent,
You've wreaked such violence   my bones all burst inside.—

—As you and I, humane,   were fused with love's deep fire,
So are we joined in pain   by eternal rancor dire;
The bone shrinks on the vein,   sinews with joints conspire;
Deranged all humors that prior   conditions could provide.—

—Sage Avicenna never,   nor Galen, Hippocrates,
The congress could dissever   of my infirmities;
They all are joined together   and make your rage increase:
I feel such catastrophes   I wish at birth I'd died.—

—Rise up, oh cursed and smitten,   you can no more delay;
Upon your brow is written   each sin we did essay:
And that to plain sight hidden   which we have done each
                                                                        day,
Must be put on display,   in view of all spread wide.—

—Who is this great lord crowned   most high king full of
                                                                        grace?
I'd sink into the ground,   such fear does he upraise;
Where could I flee unfound   by his inexorable gaze?
Earth, be my hiding place!   His wrath keep from my
                                                                        sight.—

—Lo! This is Christ our Lord,   God's only begotten Son;
To see his face tear-scored,   he loathes the fate I've spun:
We could have had reward,   his kingdom could have won;
Foul, guilty body undone,   see what we've gained by pride!
                                                [HUBERT CREEKMORE]

GUIDO GUINICELLI (1230?–1276)

Canzone of the Gentle Heart

Within the gentle heart Love shelters him,
   As birds within the green shade of the grove.
Before the gentle heart, in Nature's scheme,
   Love was not, nor the gentle heart ere Love.
      For with the sun, at once,
So sprang the light immediately; nor was
      Its birth before the sun's.
And Love hath his effect in gentleness
      Of very self; even as
Within the middle fire the heat's excess.

The fire of Love comes to the gentle heart
   Like as its virtue to a precious stone;
To which no star its influence can impart
   Till it is made a pure thing by the sun;
      For when the sun hath smit
From out its essence that which there was vile,
      The star endoweth it.
And so the heart created by God's breath
      Pure, true, and clean from guile,
A woman, like a star, enamoureth.

In gentle heart Love for like reason is
   For which the lamp's high flame is fann'd and bow'd:
Clear, piercing bright, it shines for its own bliss;
   Nor would it burn there else, it is so proud.
      For evil natures meet
With love as it were water met with flame,
      As cold abhorring heat.
Through gentle heart Love doth a track divine,—
      Like knowing like; the same
As diamond runs through iron in the mine.

The sun strikes full upon the mud all day;
   It remains vile, nor the sun's worth is less.
"By race I am gentle," the proud man doth say:
   He is the mud, the sun is gentleness.
      Let no man predicate
That aught the name of gentleness should have,
      Even in a king's estate,
Except the heart there be a gentle man's.
      The star-beam lights the wave,—
Heaven holds the star and the star's radiance.

God, in the understanding of high Heaven,
   Burns more than in our sight the living sun;
There to behold His Face unveil'd is given;
   And Heaven, whose will is homage paid to One,
      Fulfils the things which live
In God, from the beginning excellent.
      So should my lady give
That truth which in her eyes is glorified,
      On which her heart is bent,
To me whose service waiteth at her side.

My lady, God shall ask, "What dared'st thou?"
   (When my soul stands with all her acts review'd);
'Thou passed'st Heaven, into My sight, as now,
   To make Me of vain love similitude.
      To Me doth praise belong,
And to the Queen of all the realm of grace
      Who endeth fraud and wrong."
Then may I plead: "As though from Thee he came,
      Love wore an angel's face:
Lord, if I loved her, count it not my shame."
               [D. G. ROSSETTI]

RUSTICO DI FILIPPO (*c.* 1230–*c.* 1290)

Sonnet

When God had finish'd Master Messerin,
  He really thought it something to have done;
  Bird, man, and beast had got a chance in one,
And each felt flatter'd, it was hoped, therein.
For he is like a goose i' the windpipe thin,
  And like a cameleopard high i' the loins;
  To which, for manhood, you'll be told he joins
Some kinds of flesh-hues and a callow chin.
As to his singing, he affects the crow;
  As to his learning, beasts in general;
    And sets all square by dressing like a man.
God made him, having nothing else to do;
  And proved there is not anything at all
    He cannot make, if that's a thing He can.

[D. G. ROSSETTI]

GUIDO CAVALCANTI (*c.* 1255–1300)

Sonnet

Who is she that comes, makyng turn every man's eye
  And makyng the air to tremble with a bright clearnesse
  That leadeth with her love, in such nearness
No man may proffer of speech more than a sigh.
Ah God, what she is like when her owne eye turneth, is
  Fit for Amor to speake, for I can not at all;
  Such is her modesty, I would call
Every woman else but an useless uneasiness.
No one could ever tell all of her pleasauntness
  In that every high noble vertu leaneth to herward,
  So Beauty sheweth her forth as her Godhede;
Never before was our mind so high led,
  Nor have we so much of heal as will afford
  That our thought may take her immediate in its embrace.

[EZRA POUND]

To Dante

Returning from its daily quest, my Spirit
  Changed thoughts and vile in thee doth weep to find:
  It grieves me that thy mild and gentle mind
Those ample virtues which it did inherit,
Has lost. Once thou didst loathe the multitude
  Of blind and maddening men: I then loved thee—
I loved thy lofty songs, and that sweet mood
  When thou wert faithful to thyself and me.
I dare not now, through thy degraded state,
  Own the delight thy strains inspire—in vain
I seek what once thou wert—we cannot meet
  As we were wont. Again and yet again
Ponder my words: so the false Spirit shall fly,
  And leave to thee thy true integrity.

[PERCY BYSSHE SHELLEY]

Ballata

Since all my life out of my death derives,
  My joy out of despair,
  How is it, from such care,
The spirit of Love then unto passion drives?

How can I rouse my heart to love's embrace?
  It's fraught with spleen, alas!
And circled with such storm of gripping sighs
That I can summon barely voice for grace;
  And melancholy has
Despoiled its power and me would tyrannize;
While laughter, song and kindliness arise
  In me as sobs and pain.
  Behold, all men see plain
That death has mounted full into my face.

For Love, that of a like delight is born,
  Within my heart abides,
Creating from desire a being new,
But tumbles down his might in vicious scorn;
  Just so love never defied
The man who like a hireling waits his due.
Why argues he that love I should pursue?
  Only because he sees
  I pray Death for my fees
While to me every sorrow Death displays.

For heavy grief I have myself to blame
  More than man ever had:
Since Death draws to my heart another heart
Which murmurs of the cruel bitter flame
  That troubles me with sad
Concern; by which I see my virtue all depart.
A curse upon that hour when Love did start,
  Born of such quality
  That my proud life should be
Acceptable, delightful, to his ways.

[HUBERT CREEKMORE]

CECCO ANGIOLIERI, DA SIENA (*c.* 1260–*c.* 1312)

Sonnet

If I were fire, I'd burn the world away;
  If I were wind, I'd turn my storms thereon;
  If I were water, I'd soon let it drown;
If I were God, I'd sink it from the day;
If I were Pope, I'd never feel quite gay
  Until there was no peace beneath the sun;
  If I were Emperor, what would I have done?—
I'd lop men's heads all round in my own way.
If I were Death, I'd look my father up;
  If I were Life, I'd run away from him;
    And treat my mother to like calls and runs.
If I were Cecco (and that's all my hope),
  I'd pick the nicest girls to suit my whim,
    And other folk should get the ugly ones.

[D. G. ROSSETTI]

DANTE ALIGHIERI (1265–1321)

Canzone

Ladies that have intelligence in love,
  Of mine own lady I would speak with you;
  Not that I hope to count her praises through,
    But telling what I may, to ease my mind.
And I declare that when I speak thereof
  Love sheds such perfect sweetness over me
  That if my courage fail'd not, certainly
    To him my listeners must be all resign'd.
    Wherefore I will not speak in such large kind
That mine own speech should foil me, which were base;
But only will discourse of her high grace
  In these poor words, the best that I can find,
With you alone, dear dames and damozels:
'Twere ill to speak thereof with any else.

An Angel of his blessed knowledge, saith
  To God: "Lord, in the world that Thou hast made,
  A miracle in action is display'd
    By reason of a soul whose splendours fare
Even hither: and since Heaven requireth
  Nought saving her, for her it prayeth Thee,
  Thy Saints crying aloud continually."
    Yet Pity still defends our earthly share
    In that sweet soul; God answering thus the prayer:
"My well-belovèd, suffer that in peace
Your hope remain, while so My pleasure is,
  There where one dwells who dreads the loss of her;
And who in Hell unto the doom'd shall say,
'I have look'd on that for which God's chosen pray.' "

My lady is desired in the high Heaven:
   Wherefore, it now behoveth me to tell,
    Saying: Let any maid that would be well
      Esteem'd keep with her: for as she goes by,
Into foul hearts a deathly chill is driven
    By Love, that makes ill thought to perish there;
     While any who endures to gaze on her
       Must either be made noble, or else die.
      When one deserving to be raised so high
Is found, 'tis then her power attains its proof,
Making his heart strong for his soul's behoof
    With the full strength of meek humility.
Also this virtue owns she, by God's will:
Who speaks with her can never come to ill.

Love saith concerning her: "How chanceth it
    That flesh, which is of dust, should be thus pure?"
    Then, gazing always, he makes oath: "For sure,
     This is a creature of God till now unknown."
She hath that paleness of the pearl that's fit
    In a fair woman, so much and not more;
    She is as high as Nature's skill can soar;
     Beauty is tried by her comparison.
     Whatever her sweet eyes are turn'd upon,
Spirits of love do issue thence in flame,
Which through their eyes who then may look on them
    Pierce to the heart's deep chamber every one.
And in her smile Love's image you may see;
Whence none can gaze upon her steadfastly.

Dear Song, I know thou wilt hold gentle speech
  With many ladies, when I send thee forth:
  Wherefore (being mindful that thou hadst thy birth
    From Love, and art a modest, simple child),
Whomso thou meetest, say thou this to each:
  "Give me good speed! To her I wend along
  In whose much strength my weakness is made strong."
    And if, i' the end, thou wouldst not be beguiled
    Of all thy labours, seek not the defiled
And common sort; but rather choose to be
Where man and woman dwell in courtesy.
    So to the road thou shalt be reconciled,
And find the lady, and with the lady, Love.
Commend thou me to each, as doth behove.

[D. G. ROSSETTI]

Sonnet

Mine eyes beheld the blessed pity spring
  Into thy countenance immediately
  A while agone, when thou beheld'st in me
The sickness only hidden grief can bring;
And then I knew thou wast considering
  How abject and forlorn my life must be;
  And I became afraid that thou shouldst see
My weeping, and account it a base thing.
Therefore I went out from thee; feeling how
  The tears were straightway loosen'd at my heart
  Beneath thine eyes' compassionate control.
  And afterwards I said within my soul:
"Lo! with this lady dwells the counterpart
Of the same Love who holds we weeping now."

[D. G. ROSSETTI]

To Guido Cavalcanti

Guido, I would that Lapo, thou, and I,
   Led by some strong enchantment, might ascend
   A magic ship, whose charmèd sails should fly
   With winds at will, where'er our thoughts might wend,
And that no change, nor any evil chance,
   Should mar our joyous voyage; but it might be
   That even satiety should still enhance
   Between our hearts their strict community,
And that the bounteous wizard then would place
   Vanna and Bice and my gentle love,
   Companions of our wandering, and would grace
With passionate talk, wherever we might rove,
   Our time, and each were as content and free
   As I believe that thou and I should be.

                    [PERCY BYSSHE SHELLEY]

Canzone

The eyes that weep for pity of the heart
   Have wept so long that their grief languisheth
      And they have no more tears to weep withal:
And now, if I would ease me of a part
   Of what, little by little, leads to death,
      It must be done by speech, or not at all.
   And because often, thinking, I recall
How it was pleasant, ere she went afar,
   To talk of her with you, kind damozels,
   I talk with no one else,
But only with such hearts as women's are.
   And I will say,—still sobbing as speech fails,—
That she hath gone to Heaven suddenly,
And hath left Love below, to mourn with me.

Beatrice is gone up into high Heaven,
   The kingdom where the angels are at peace;
     And lives with them; and to her friends is dead.
Not by the frost of winter was she driven
   Away, like others; nor by summer-heats;
     But through a perfect gentleness, instead.
     For from the lamp of her meek lowlihead
Such an exceeding glory went up hence
   That it woke wonder in the Eternal Sire,
     Until a sweet desire
Enter'd Him for that lovely excellence,
   So that He bade her to Himself aspire:
Counting this weary and most evil place
Unworthy of a thing so full of grace.

Wonderfully out of the beautiful form
   Soar'd her clear spirit, waxing glad the while;
     And is in its first home, there where it is.
Who speaks thereof, and feels not the tears warm
   Upon his face, must have become so vile
     As to be dead to all sweet sympathies.
     Out upon him! an abject wretch like this
May not imagine anything of her,—
   He needs no bitter tears for his relief.
     But sighing comes, and grief,
And the desire to find no comforter
   (Save only Death, who makes all sorrow brief),
To him who for a while turns in his thought
How she hath been among us, and is not.

With sighs my bosom always laboureth
  On thinking, as I do continually,
    Of her for whom my heart now breaks apace;
And very often when I think of death,
  Such a great inward longing comes to me
    That it will change the colour of my face;
    And, if the idea settles in its place,
All my limbs shake as with an ague-fit;
  Till, starting up in wild bewilderment,
  I do become so shent
That I go forth, lest folk misdoubt of it.
  Afterward, calling with a sore lament
On Beatrice, I ask, "Canst thou be dead?"
And calling on her, I am comforted.

Grief with its tears, and anguish with its sighs,
  Come to me now whene'er I am alone;
    So that I think the sight of me gives pain.
And what my life hath been, that living dies,
  Since for my lady the New Birth's begun,
    I have not any language to explain.
    And so, dear ladies, though my heart were fain,
I scarce could tell indeed how I am thus.
  All joy is with my bitter life at war;
  Yea, I am fallen so far
That all men seem to say, "Go out from us,"
  Eyeing my cold white lips, how dead they are.
But she, though I be bow'd unto the dust,
Watches me; and will guerdon me, I trust.

Weep, piteous Song of mine, upon thy way,
  To the dames going, and the damozels,
    For whom, and for none else,
Thy sisters have made music many a day.
Thou, that art very sad and not as they,
  Go dwell thou with them as a mourner dwells.

                  [D. G. ROSSETTI]

The Banquet: Dissertation 2, Canzone 1

Ye intelligences, turning the third sphere,
Hear out the reasoning within my heart
Stranger than I can openly relate.
The heaven that obeys your moving art
—Such noble natures as you surely are—
I see has brought me to my present state;
So of my suffering any debate
Seems that it rightly should be told to ye:
Wherefore I pray that ye will hear my part.
I would tell the strange history of the heart,
How the sad soul there weeps bitterly
Because a spirit speaks, opposing her,
That comes upon the shining of your star.

My sorrowful heart's life often would be
A thought so sweet that it would rise in flight
Many a time to the feet of our great Sire
To see a Lady glorious in light,
Of whom it spoke so blessedly to me
That my soul spoke, and said: "I would go there."
But, putting her to flight, one does appear
Who lords it with such power over me,
My trembling heart shows outwardly its fear.
And this one made me see a Lady here,
And said: "Who would behold felicity,
Let him look in this Lady's eyes
If he fears not the agony of sighs."

Now comes the adversary, who can slay,
Against my humble thought that would give me
Word of an angel crowned in the skies,
So that my soul cried out, and still must cry,
Saying: "Alas, how is she fled away,
The piteous one who showed my pity's guise."
Then this afflicted heart said of its eyes:
"What hour such a lady looked therein,
Why would they not believe my word of her?"
Always I said: "In such eyes as hers are
One surely stands whose glance can murder men.
It not availed me, that I saw it plain,
Against their gazing whereby I am slain."

"You are not slain, but only as though blind,
Soul in our keeping, with so great lament,"
A spirit of gentle love replied to me.
"Because, upon that Lady all intent,
The life has so been driven from your mind
That you are full of fear, and cowardly.
But she is pity and humility,
Courteous and wise in her magnificence:
Know that she is your Lady from this day!
And having undeceived your eyes you may
See such high miracles her ornaments
That you will say to Love: O my true Lord,
Behold thy handmaiden, who will do thy word."

Song, I think they will be few indeed
Who well and rightly understand your sense.
So difficult your speech and intricate.
Wherefore if you should come by any chance
Among such folk so little fit to read
As that you seem not to *communicate*,
I'd have you take heart even at that rate,
My latest and dear one, saying to them:
"Look you at least how beautiful I am."

[HOWARD NEMEROV]

All Ye That Pass

All ye that pass along Love's trodden way,
Pause ye awhile and say
  If there be any grief like unto mine:
I pray you that you hearken a short space
Patiently, if my case
  Be not a piteous marvel and a sign.

Love (never, certes, for my worthless part,
But of his own great heart)
  Vouchsafed to me a life so calm and sweet
That oft I heard folk question as I went
What such great gladness meant:—
  They spoke of it behind me in the street.

But now that fearless bearing is all gone
  Which with Love's hoarded wealth was given me;
  Till I am grown to be
So poor that I have dread to think thereon.

And thus it is that I, being like as one
  Who is ashamed and hides his poverty,
  Without seem full of glee,
And let my heart within travail and moan.

                                    [D. G. ROSSETTI]

Sonnet to the Lady Pietra

My curse be on the day when first I saw
   The brightness in those treacherous eyes of thine,—
The hour when from my heart thou cam'st to draw
   My soul away, that both might fail and pine—
   My curse be on the skill that smooth'd each line
Of my vain songs,—the music and just law
   Of art, by which it was my dear design
That the whole world should yield thee love and awe.
Yea, let me curse mine own obduracy,
   Which firmly holds what doth itself confound—
     To wit, thy fair perverted face of scorn:
     For whose sake Love is oftentimes forsworn
So that men mock at him; but most at me
   Who would hold fortune's wheel and turn it round.

[D. G. ROSSETTI]

CINO DA PISTOIA (c. 1270–1337)

Desperate

All things that please another displease me;
   The whole world brings disgust; it's gone awry.
   —Now then, what pleases you?—I will reply:
   When someone knifes another, fast and free;
And stroke of sword it is I'm pleased to see
   In some one else's face, ships sinking nigh:
   I'd like to be a second Nero, I
   Could wish each woman ugly as can be.
Good cheer, amusement please me as a rule;
   And melancholy pleases me as well:
   And every day I'd like to chase a fool,
And pay my court to Sorrow for a spell,
   And then to kill all those, all those I kill
   In my proud thoughts where I find death at will.

[L. R. LIND]

FOLGORE DA SAN GEMINIANO (*c.* 1270–*c.* 1330)

March

In March I give you plenteous fisheries
  Of lamprey and of salmon, eel and trout
  Dental and dolphin, sturgeon, all the rout
Of fish in all the streams that fill the seas.
With fishermen and fishing-boats at ease,
  Sail-barques and arrow-barques and galleons stout,
  To bear you, while the season lasts, far out,
And back, through spring, to any port you please.
But with fair mansions see that it be fill'd,
  With everything exactly to your mind,
    And every sort of comfortable folk.
No convent suffer there, nor priestly guild:
  Leave the mad monks to preach after their kind
    Their scanty truth, their lies beyond a joke.

                    [D. G. ROSSETTI]

May

I give you horses for your games in May,
  And all of them well-train'd unto the course,—
  Each docile, swift, erect, a goodly horse;
With armour on their chests, and bells at play
Between their brows, and pennons fair and gay;
  Fine nets, and housings meet for warriors,
  Emblazon'd with the shields ye claim for yours,
Gules, argent, or, all dizzy at noonday.
And spears shall split, and fruit go flying up
In merry counterchange for wreaths that drop
  From balconies and casements far above;
And tender damsels with young men and youths
Shall kiss together on the cheeks and mouths;
  And every day be glad with joyful love.

                    [D. G. ROSSETTI]

FRANCESCO PETRARCH (1304–1374)

Against the Court of Rome

Vengeaunce must fall on thee, thou filthie whore
Of Babilon, thou breaker of Christ's fold,
That from achorns, and from the water colde,
Art riche become with making many poore,
Thou treason's neste that in thy harte dost holde
Of cankard malice, and of myschief more
Than pen can wryte, or may with tongue be tolde,
Slave to delights that chastitie hath solde;
For wyne and ease which settith all thy store
Uppon whoredome and none other lore,
In thy pallais of strompetts yonge and olde
Theare walks Plentie, and Belzebub thy Lorde
Guydes thee and them, and doth thy raigne upholde:
It is but late, as wryting will recorde,
That poore thou weart withouten lande or golde;
Yet now hathe golde and pryde, by one accorde,
In wickednesse so spread thy lyf abrode,
That it dothe stincke before the face of God.

[SIR THOMAS WYATT]

Canzone

It is the evening hour; the rapid sky
   Bends westward; and the hasty daylight flees
   To some new land, some strange expectant race.
   An old and weary pilgrim-woman sees
   The lonely foreign desert-dark draw nigh.
   Fearful, she urges on her stumbling pace.
   And to her resting-place
   At length she comes, and knows
   The sweetness of repose;
   The pains of pilgrimage, the road's duress
   Fade in enveloping forgetfulness.
   But oh, alas, my hurts that ache by day
   Are but more pitiless
   When the light sinks into the west away.

When the sun's burning wheels have sped along,
   And night pursues, rolling its deepest black
   From highest peaks into the sheltered plain,
   The sober woodsman slings upon his back
   His tools, and sings his artless mountain-song,
   Discharging on the air his load of pain.
   And yet his only gain
   Is, on his humble board,
   The food the woods afford,
   Acorns, which poets honor, yet abjure.
   Let him be happy, let him sleep secure,
   Though I no happiness have ever won,
   No rest, no ease, no cure,
   For all the turning of the stars and sun.

And when the shepherd sees the evening shade
  Rising and graying o'er the eastward land,
  And the sun dropping to its nightly nest,
  He rises; takes his well-worn crook in hand;
  And leaves the grass, the spring, the beechen glade,
  And quietly leads the tired flock to its rest.
  He finds a cave, recessed
  In crags, wherein to spread
  Green branches for his bed,
  And there he sleeps, untroubled, solitary.
  But then, O cruel Love, the more you harry
  My breaking strength to that most hopeless chase
  Of her who flees apace,
  And Love will never aid to noose the quarry.

In the sea's vales the sailors on their bark
  Throw down their limbs on the hard boards to sleep
  When the sun dips beneath the western main.
  Oh, though he hide within the farthest deep,
  And leave Morocco's mountains to the dark,
  Granada and the Pillars and all Spain,
  And though the worldwide pain
  Of suffering man and beast
  In the first light have ceased,
  There comes no night with mercy to conclude
  My ardor, ever in suffering renewed.
  My love grows old; soon shall my captor see me
  Ten years in servitude.
  And still no saviour comes with strength to free me!

And as I seek with words my wounds to numb,
  I watch at eve the unyoked oxen turning
  In from the fields, down from the furrowed hill.
  My yoke, alas, is never lifted from
  My shoulders, and my hurts are ever burning,
  And in my eyes the tears are springing still.
  Alas, it was my will
  To carve the unearthly grace
  Of her most lovely face
  In the immutable matter of my heart.
  Now it is carved so deep that strength nor art
  May rub it thence until that final day
  When soul and body part.
  Even then, perhaps, it will not pass away.

O my unhappy song,
  My grief has made you grieve,
  You will not dare to leave
  My heart to show your sorrows anywhere;
  And yet, for others' praise you shall not care,
  For all your burden is the weight of pain
  Left by the flames that flare
  From the cold rock to which I cling, in vain.

                     [MORRIS BISHOP]

Complaint of a Lover Rebuked

Love, that liveth and reigneth in my thought,
  That built his seat within my captive breast,
Clad in the arms wherein with me he fought,
  Oft in my face he doth his banner rest.
She, that me taught to love, and suffer pain:
  My doubtful hope and eke my hot desire
With shamefaced cloak to shadow and restrain;
  Her smiling grace converteth straight to ire,
And coward Love then to the heart apace
  Taketh his flight, whereas he lurks, and plains
His purpose lost, and dare not show his face.
  For my lord's guilt thus faultless bide I pains;
Yet from my lord shall not my foot remove;
Sweet is his death, that takes his end by love.

                [THE EARL OF SURREY]

The Nightingale

That nightingale, whose strain so sweetly flows
  Mourning her ravish'd young or much-lov'd mate,
  A soothing charm o'er all the valleys throws
  And skies, with notes well-tun'd to her sad state:
And all the night she seems my kindred woes
  With me to weep and on my sorrows wait;
  Sorrows that from my own fond fancy rose,
  Who deem'd a goddess could not yield to fate.
How easy to deceive who sleeps secure!
  Who could have thought that to dull earth would turn
  Those eyes that as the sun shone bright and pure?
Ah! now what fortune wills I see full sure:
  That loathing life yet living I should see
  How few its joys, how little they endure!

                [THOMAS LEMESURIER]

GIOVANNI BOCCACCIO (1313–1375)

Apology For Love

Old as I am, for ladies' love unfit,
The power of beauty I remember yet,
Which once inflam'd my soul, and still inspires my wit.
If love be folly, the severe divine
Has felt that folly, though he censures mine;
Pollutes the pleasures of a chaste embrace,
Acts what I write, and propagates in grace,
With riotous excess, a priestly race.
Suppose him free, and that I forge the offence,
He show'd the way, perverting first my sense:
In malice witty, and with venom fraught,
He makes me speak the things I never thought.
Compute the gains of his ungovern'd zeal;
Ill suits his cloth the praise of railing well.
The world will think that what we loosely write,
Though now arraign'd, he read with some delight
Because he seems to chew the cud again,
When his broad comment wakes the text too plain;
And teaches more in one explaining page,
Than all the double meanings of the stage.
   What needs he paraphrase on what we mean?
We were at worst but wanton; he's obscene.
I, nor my fellows, nor myself excuse;
But love's the subject of the comic muse:
Nor can we write without it, nor would you
A tale of only dry instruction view.
Nor love is always of a vicious kind,
But oft to virtuous acts inflames the mind,
Awakes the sleepy vigor of the soul,
And, brushing o'er, adds motion to the pool.
Love, studious how to please, improves our parts
With polish'd manners, and adorns with arts.

Love first invented verse, and form'd the rhyme,
The motion measur'd, harmoniz'd the chime;
To liberal acts enlarg'd the narrow-soul'd,
Soften'd the fierce, and made the coward bold:
The world, when waste, he peopled with increase,
And warring nations reconcil'd in peace.

[JOHN DRYDEN]

Sonnet

Now perish, Baïa, root and stock and name:
  May a bleak wilderness blot out thy shore
  And from thy fountains let pure venom pour,
  And bathers nevermore thy sands acclaim.
May woe and grief replace each sport and game
  And sailors shun thy port forevermore:
  Down from thy skies that smiled in days of yore
  May lightning fall and smoke and sulphur flame.
For thou with thy licentiousness hast made
  Corrupt the chastest heart of womankind—
  If my eyes told me true not long ago.
Now all my life I'll grieve as one betrayed,
  In foolish fondness ignorant and blind—
  Ah would I had been blind not long ago!

[T. G. BERGIN]

Welsh

The Celtic languages, of which the most important are Welsh and Irish, are not related to the Germanic or the Latin-Romance tongues whose poetry makes up the bulk of this volume. Neither do they share, in their early and medieval periods, anything in common with the poetry or culture of the other countries of Europe, though by the end of that era some traces of Latin, Provençal and French influence can be discerned. There are, rather naturally, parallels in the poetry of Wales and Ireland, mainly in the fresh observation and love of nature, and in the bardic tradition.

A specific difference, and one distinct also from all other literatures, has been aptly described by Gwyn Williams in his The Burning Tree *(p. 15). Welsh poetry, he writes, is not in the tradition of Greece and Rome, attempting a structure like a classic temple; rather, it uses a dispersion of themes interwoven like the stone circles of ancient forts or the designs on Celtic crosses. This tradition remains valid throughout Welsh literature down to the present day.*

Beginning in the sixth century with Aneirin's Gododdin, *a series of*

elegies on the warriors in the battle of Catraeth, the literature of Wales
has one of the longest continuous traditions of Europe. The two brief
poems given here cannot do justice to the quality of the much longer,
more involved and moving, laments—the combination of vigor, joy,
beauty of nature with the imminence of war and death. With the
exception of the surprising playfulness of the poem for Dinogad, a grim
brooding, similar to that in the Anglo-Saxon "The Seafarer," hangs
over much of the earliest poetry.

   Aneirin, Taliesin and others of the bards were often soldiers as
well as poets, and knew their patrons both in battle crises and around the
festive tables at home. It was their duty to praise the patrons' virtues
in life and express the mourning of the community at death. They
had a keen interest in technical matters, and like their counterparts
in Ireland, made heavy use of alliteration, assonance and interplay of
rhymes to heighten effects. The Welsh in particular evolved complicated
systems of meters and stanzas. In the death laments, exaggerated
emotion was the prevailing tone, dictated by the official nature of the
occasion. A pleasant exception to this is Lewis Glyn Cothi's poem on the
death of his son. Here the simplicity of the grief comes through as if
in genuine keening, and the details of childhood, so unusual in all
medieval writing, increase its moving power.

   The greatest poet of this era in Wales, and indeed one of the greatest
in all Europe, is Dafydd ap Gwilym. His nature and love poems are
vigorous, humorous and beautiful, overflowing with daring metaphors
and images, and full of technical brilliance. Since comparatively few
people can read Welsh and there are few palatable translations of his
work, he has hardly received the international popular fame he deserves.

   He and other poets of his time betray slight traces of Troubadour
and Trouvère writing, whose influence had reached Wales through the
conquering Normans, but none of them were bound by the conventions.
Their own native poetry swallowed up the imported artifice in a torrent
of vivid imagery, tumbling word compounds, powerful or dancing
cadences and true feeling.

ANEIRIN (6th century)

Of Manly Disposition

Of manly disposition was the youth,
Valor had he in the tumult;
Fleet thick-maned chargers
Were under the thigh of the illustrious youth;
A shield, bright and broad,
Was on the slender swift flank,
A sword, blue and bright,
Golden spurs, and ermine.
It is not by me
That hatred shall be shown to thee;
I will do better towards thee,
To celebrate thee in poetic eulogy.
Sooner hadst thou gone to the bloody bier
Than to the nuptial feast;
Sooner hadst thou gone to be food for ravens
Than to the conflict of spears;
Thou beloved friend of Owain!
Wrong it is that he should be under ravens.
It is evident in what region
The only son of Marro was killed.

[D. S. EVANS]

The Lost Legion

Together arise the associated warriors.
Strangers to the country, their deeds shall be heard of.
There was slaughtering with axes and blades,
And there was raising of large cairns over the men of toil.

Together arise the warriors, together met,
And all with one accord sallied forth;
Short were their lives, long is the grief of those who loved them.
Seven times their number of Lloegrians they had slain;
After the conflict women raised a lamentation;
Many a mother has the tear on her eyelash.

[D. S. EVANS]

TALIESIN (6th century)

Dialogue between Poet and Patron

—A horseman resorts to the city,
With his white dogs, and large horns;
I, who have not before seen thee, know thee not.
  —A horseman resorts to the river's mouth,
On a stout and warlike steed;
Come with me, let me not be refused.
  —I will not go that way at present;
Bear with the conduct of the delayer;
And may the blessing of heaven and earth come upon thee.
  —Thou, who hast not seen me daily,
And who resemblest a prudent man,
How long wilt thou absent thyself, and when wilt thou come?
  —When I return from Caer Seon,
From contending with Jews,
I will come to the city of Lleu and Gwidion.
  —Come with me into the city,
Thou shalt have wine which I have set apart,
And pure gold on thy clasp.
  —I know not the confident man,
Who owns a fire and a couch;
Fairly and sweetly dost thou speak.
  —Come with me to my dwelling,
Thou shalt have high foaming wine.
My name is Ugnach, the son of Mydno.
  —Ugnach a blessing on thy throne!
And mayst thou have grace and honor!
I am Taliesin who will repay thee thy banquet.
  —Taliesin, chief of men,
Victor in the contest of song,
Remain here until Wednesday.
  —Ugnach! the most affluent in riches,
Grace be to thee from the highest region;
I will not deserve blame; I will not tarry.

[D. S. EVANS]

ANONYMOUS (7th century)

For Little Dinogad

Full is Dinogad's petticoat, see!
Of martens' fur it was made by me.
Whistle, whistle, and whistle again,
Then we'll sing, O a lusty strain:
When your daddy went a-hunting, to fetch good cheer,
A staff in his hand, on his shoulder a spear,
To his dogs so swift he'd whistle and sing—
"Giff, Gaff, catch him then, catch him and bring!"
Deftly the fish from his coracle he'd spear
As a lion leaps when he kills the deer.
When your daddy a-hunting to the mountain would go,
He'd bring you back a wild boar, a stag, or a roe,
He'd bring you back a grouse, as speckled as you'd wish,
From the Falls of Derwennydd he'd bring you a fish.
Whatever came running within his spear's throw,
Were it fox or wild cat or great wild boar,
Unless it had wings it would run no more.

[H. IDRIS BELL]

HYWEL AB OWAIN GWYNEDD (1140–1170)

A Love Poem

My chosen she is, my bright, dainty darling,
  Tall and white in her wimple of purple hue.
And my chosen joy is to watch her, so womanly,
  When scarce heard she utters her seemly speech.
And my chosen part is to share her company,
  Exchanging in secret love's gift, love's thrill.
  The choice that I make, thou wave-white wonder,
  Thou wise among women, is the fine Welsh thou speakest.
My chosen art thou; to thee what am I?
  Ah! why art thou silent, though fair is thy silence?
Such a maid I have chosen I can never repent it;
  'Tis rightly one chooseth so choice a beauty.

[H. IDRIS BELL]

GRUFFUDD AB YR YNAD COCH (13th century)

The Death of Llywelyn ap Gruffudd

The heart is cold under a breast of pitiful fear
   for a king, the oaken door of Aberffraw.
Fine gold was paid to us from his hand
and he deserved the golden chaplet.
Golden horns of a golden king do not bring me the joy
   of Llywelyn; I am not free to arm as I would.
Woe to me for my lord, the unshamed hawk,
   woe for the calamity of his bringing down.
Woe for the loss, woe for the destiny,
   woe for the news that he has a wound.
Cadwaladr of defence, protection's sharp piercer,
   he of the red spear, golden-handed ruler,
he shared out wealth, every winter he dressed me
   in the garments he had worn.
Lord of great herds, there's no more prospering,
but for him there remains eternal life.
My wrath's on the Englishman for despoiling me;
mine is it now to bewail death's need.
I have cause to speak harshly with God
   who has left me without him.
Mine is it to praise without stint or stop,
mine is it from now on long to remember him.
All my life long my grief will be for him;
   since the grief is mine, mine is the weeping.
I've lost a lord and I grasp a long fear,
for a hand has killed the lord of the court.
O good true Lord, listen to me,
how loud I bewail; woe to the wailing!
Lord of armies before the killing of the eighteen,
liberal lord, lone hero ordering battle,
brave lord, like a lion directing the world,
   a lord always restless to destroy,
lord of lucky ventures, before leaving his splendor;
   no Englishman would dare to wound him.

A lord who was roofstone where the Welsh gather,
   of the line which should hold sway in Aberffraw.
Lord Christ, how grieved I am for him!
O true Lord, release me with him.
His fall came from the heavy sword-stroke,
from the long swords crushing him down.
By the wound on my king I am dismayed
and the news of the weariness of Bodfaeo's lord.
A complete man was killed by a hostile hand;
   every privilege of old age sprang from him,
candle of kingship, strong lion of Gwynedd,
   chair of honor; there was need of him.
For the death of all Britain, a deathsong for the leader,
for the killing of Nancoel's lion, of Nancaw's shield.
Many a sliding tear runs down the cheek,
   many a flank is red and torn,
much blood has soaked about the feet,
many a widow shrieks for him,
many a sad mind now breaks down,
many a son's left fatherless,
many a homestead stained in the fire's path
   and many a wilderness left by the plunderer,
many a piteous cry, as once at Camlan,
many a tear has fallen down the cheek!
For the killing of our prop, our golden-handed king,
for Llywelyn's death, I remember no one.
The heart is chilled under a breast of fear,
lust shrivels like dry branches.
See you not the way of the wind and the rain?
See you not the oaks beat together?
See you not the sea stinging the land?
   See you not the truth equipping?
See you not the sun sailing the sky?
   See you not the stars have fallen?
Do you not believe God, demented men?
   See you not the end of existence?

A sigh to you, God, that the sea may come over the land!
  Why are we left to linger?
There's no retreat from the prison of fear,
there's nowhere to dwell, alas for the dwelling!
There is no counsel, no lock, no opening,
  no way of delivery from terror's sad counsel.
Each retinue was worthy of him
and every warrior stayed about him,
every dogged one swore by his hand,
every ruler, every province was his;
every district, every homestead's unsettled,
every clan and line now falls.
The weak and strong were kept by his hand,
every child now weeps in his cradle.
Little good it did me to be tricked
into leaving my head on, with no head on him.
A head which, falling, made panic welcome;
a head which, falling, made it better to give up;
a soldier's head, a head for praise henceforth;
a leader's head, a dragon's head was on him,
head of fair, dogged Llywelyn; it shocks the world
  that an iron stake should pierce it.
My lord's head, a harsh-falling pain is mine,
my soul's head, which has no memorial;
a head which owned honor in nine hundred lands,
  with the homage of nine hundred feasts;
a king's head, iron flew from his hand;
a king's head, a proud hawk breaching a gap;
a regal head of a thrusting wolf,
a king's head this; may Heaven be its refuge!
A magnificent lord, a blessed host with him;
proud sustainer of the Breton voyage.
True regal king of Aberffraw,
may Heaven's white kingdom be his abode!

[GWYN WILLIAMS]

DAFYDD AP GWILYM (*fl.* 1340–70)

To the Nun

For a girl dark-eyed, pale-faced,
With love dolour I daily waste.
How fond am I, dear God, to pine
For her who never will be mine!
Is't true, maid whom I most love,
That you contemn the birch grove,
Whilst to your cloister close you cling,
Eight-hued star, with your psalm-singing?
A saint, a votaress you are,
Darling of all the virgin choir;
Yet why, o' God's name, why so wed
To your cress and water and dry bread?
Nay, leave your beads, your prayers, and break
With Rome's sour creed, for Mary's sake;
Quit your cell for the green glade,
For Spring suits ill to the nun's trade,
And your religion, dearest dear,
To our lord Love is treason clear.
Mantle, green gown, and spousal ring
Were seemlier raiment for the Spring.
Come you then to the whispering birch
And the young leaves, the cuckoo's church,
Where no churl will say us nay
Though we win heaven in the woods of May.
From overmuch religion free,
Con your Ovid heedfully,
Among the woodbines we will win
A woodland shrift from every sin.
The saints, believe me, and God above
Are well minded to pardon love.
Is it worse for a high-born maid
To save her soul in the forest glade
Than if we had done even as they
Who at Rome or Santiago pray?   [H. IDRIS BELL]

A Snowy Day

I cannot sleep or take the air—
Of a truth this load is hard to bear!
Ford or slope is none to be found,
Nor open space, nor bare ground.
No girl's word shall tempt me now
Out of my house into the snow.
The plaguey feathers drifting down
Like dragon's scales cling to the gown,
And all I wear would soon be
White as miller's coat to see.
True 'tis, the Winter Calends gone,
Ermine's the wear for everyone;
In January's month, first of the year,
God makes hermits everywhere.
Everywhere, the country round,
He has whitewashed the black ground,
Clothed in white each woodland glade,
On every copse a white sheet spread.
To every stump clings heavenly meal,
Like the white blossoms of April.
A cold veil on the forest lies,
A load of chalk crushes the trees.
Like wheaten flour the drifts appear,
A coat of mail that the plains wear,
A cold grit on field and fallow,
On earth's whole skin a thick tallow,
Foam-flakes flying thick and fast,
Fleeces big as a man's fist,
White bees of heaven on the wing,
Through all Gwynedd wandering.
Will God's plenty never cease—
So many feathers of holy geese,
Like winnowed chaff, heaped together,
A robe of ermine above the heather?

There in deep drifts the fine dust stays,
Where song was and the winding ways.
Who can tell me what folk they are
On the wintry earth spit from afar?
Heaven's white angels they must be
Busy about their carpentry.
The plank is lifted from the flour bin,
And down floats the flour within;
Silver cloaks of ice that pass,
Quicksilver, the coldest ever was,
A hampering chimer, white and chill,
Cement on hollow, ditch, and hill,
Earth's mail corselet, cold and hard,
A pavement vast as the sea's graveyard.
On all my land what monstrous fall,
From sea to sea a gray wall!
Who dare affront its rude domain?
A cloak of lead!—where is the rain?

[H. IDRIS BELL]

The Seagull

A white seagull on the breast of the sea.
Surely as perfect in beauty is she
As the white snow or the whiter moon,
A glove of the sea, gleaned from the sun.
Proud and swift when she fishes and light
Over the waves of the sea in her flight.
O white, white bird, we will go, you and I,
Your hand in my hand, the lily of the sea.
A white nun on the wave's crest you lie,
Your white veil all brightness as paper might be.
But bend your course a little for me,
And that castle, white bird, you may chance to see,
Where a lovely lady sits watching all day,
More lovely than Eigr; go to her, say
How much I desire her, how much would give
If she would choose me, with me to live.
If herself should come, then greet her so,
As deftly as any wise servant should know;
And say, my elegant messenger,
I am like to die if I win not her.
O brother men! O perfect love!
Did such love Taliesin move?
Did Merddin who was all desire
Love fairer woman with such fire?
My lady excelling bears copper hair,
That oats and barley seem harvested there,
And if you see when thither come
The loveliest cheek in Christendom,
O gull, bring welcome back with you,
Or else this heart will break in two.

[DAVID BELL]

He Desires Her Husband's Death

I love her always; in that is my pain.
When she I love scorns me to love is but vain.
She's the beauty of Iseult, but to Jealousy wed;
A lasting passion on her I've laid.
But I, being poor, can never win
So perfect a lady, nor call her mine.
I shall not win my fine-browed dear,
For her jealous husband lets no one near,
And when she comes out with the people to walk
The wretch comes with her to watch her talk.
But let not that dunghill, Jealousy,
Think that all his own she'll be!

For Jealousy drives mirth away
With his bitter face; he despises play.
The cuckoo nor the nightingale,
Nor linnet more than fox can call
His love, nor the dark woods in truth,
Nor song, nor hazel nuts of youth,
Nor all the singing birds of May.
The young green leaves him cold as clay.
The chatter of thrush in the green leaves
With the proud nightingale but grieves
Sour Jealousy; a hateful thing
To him the hounds and the harp-string.
For Jealousy is Ireland's son;
So much I hate not any one.

Let Gwen, because 'tis I who love her
And her white brow this long time, remove her
Within six months from his jealous bed;
For I love best the married maid.

Oh, but earth and stones I'd see
And the rod on the white one's husband lie
And the weight of eight hired oxen laid
In turves upon the churl's damned head.

Of my estate I would concede
His length of earth to see him dead,
And that the maiden I might have
I'd see a cross upon his grave,
In the cold trench his winding sheet
And coffin of yellow alder set.
My God! if this thing I might have,
Another month he should not live.
To see him dead she would be glad.
I should be glad to see him dead.   [DAVID BELL]

LEWIS GLYN COTHI (15th century)

On the Death of his Son

One son was a jewel to me:
o Dwynwen, his father bewails his birth!
I have been left pain for love,
to ache for ever without a son.
My plaything is dead and my sides
are sick for Siôn y Glyn.[1]
I moan continually
for a little story-book chieftain.
A sweet apple and a bird
the boy loved, and white pebbles,
a bow made of a thorn twig
and little brittle swords of wood.
He feared a pipe and a scarecrow
and begged his mother for a ball.
He'd sing for anyone,
singing io-o for a nut.

[1] Siôn is pronounced "Shone."

He'd make as though to flatter
and then fall out with me;
then make it up for a chip of wood
or a dice that he desired.
O, that Siôn, sweet innocent,
could live again like Lazarus.
Beuno brought seven heaven-dwellers
back again into this life.
Woe upon woe to my true heart
that Siôn's soul does not make eight.
O Mary, woe for his lying down
and woe to my side for his grave!
Siôn's death stands near me
like two barbs in my breast.
My son, child of my hearth,
my breast, my heart, my song,
my one delight before my death,
my knowing poet, my luxury.
my jewel, and my candle,
my sweet soul, my one betrayal,
my chick learning my song,
my chaplet of Iseult, my kiss,
my nest, (woe that he's gone!)
my lark, my little wizard.
My Siôn, my bow, my arrow,
my suppliant, my boyhood,
Siôn who sends to his father
a sharpness of longing and love.
No more smiles for my lips,
no more laughter from my mouth,
no more sweet entertainment,
no more begging for nuts,
no longer any playing ball
and no more singing aloud.
Farewell, whilst I live below,
my merry darling, my Siôn.

[GWYN WILLIAMS]

Irish

*P*oetry in Old Irish begins in the sixth century with work of uncertain authorship and later swells to a flood of anonymous nature poems. In the ninth century the prose heroic cycles and mythological and historical tales were being composed, but by about 1200 were tending to change into a ballad type of narrative, or to incorporate poems into the text. About this time the bardic tradition developed with much the same characteristics as the Welsh praise-poetry, and continued into the seventeenth century.

Most of the poets whose work can be definitely linked with a name are bards. Donnachadh mor O'Dala is one of these, though the poem here is not typically bardic. The major part of the poetry, however, is anonymous, and the best of it is nature poetry—isolated productions or verses imbedded in the sagas. "May" and "Summer Is Gone" belong to the Finn Cycle; "Fand Yields . . ." to the Cu Chulainn Cycle. There is also a body of religious verse that is not without charm, and epigrams and longer works with a strong tendency to satire.

Though love of nature and the sensuous description of it are the *chief glories of this early poetry, personal emotion and a wild exhilarating imagination are nearly as prominent. The warm domestic picture of the scholar and his cat, Pangur Ban (White Pangur), and the fantasy of Mad Sweeney flying like a bird through the trees are only slight indications of the riches.*

A word about the Sweeney poem—it is from Suibne Geilt, *a prose romance with occasional verses. Of the sixty-five stanzas of his song of the trees, thirty-two, mostly interpolated reminiscence, are omitted. Sweeney went mad in the battle of Mag Rath* (A.D. 639) *after he had outraged St. Ronan Finn—either by throwing his psalter into a lake, or casting a spear at him—and the saint had cursed him: "You may have leave to go with the birds." And Sweeney did, forthwith. The poem here occurs when he has recovered his reason, but been driven mad again by an inquisitive hag, who then flies through the trees after him, pursuing much as the Furies did Orestes. One legend says he died, as in the next to last stanza, by an antler point, placed so it would pierce him when he leaned over to drink.*

As in the early Welsh, this Irish poetry is still untrammelled by outside influences. And it shares the indigenous Celtic taste for alliteration, complex patterns of rhyme and assonance, and rigid stanza forms.

ANONYMOUS (8th century)

In Praise of Aed, the Chieftain

Kindler of glory's embers,
Aed, goodly hand of giving;
Comeliest that song remembers
By pastoral Roeriu living.

A mighty shaft and loyal
Whom glory overarches;
Of all men else most royal
In grassy Maistiu's marches.

My love—if such his pleasure—
To Dermot's son I bring it;
My song—more worth than treasure—
To his high praise I sing it.

Dear name! renowned in story,
Aed! no man may decry him;
Where Liffey flows in glory
Fame's voice shall ne'er bely him.

Grandchild of that fierce fighter
Muireach, a cliff of splendours,
Honor—no fame is brighter—
To his race Cualu renders.

A stately tree, a glowing
Jewel whom strife embolden;
A silver sapling growing
From soil of princes olden.

Songs at the alefeast ringing,
Scales climbed of comely measures,
Bards with their heady singing
Acclaim Aed and his pleasures.   [ROBIN FLOWER]

ANONYMOUS (9th century)

Four Short Poems

A trip to Rome—great pains and little gain!
　　That King you seek, so dear—
Unless you bring Him with you, all too plain
　　You will not find Him here.

*　　　*　　　*

　　I don't know with exactly whom
　　　　Edan will sleep, I own;
　　I do know, though, that fair Edan
　　　　Will not be sleeping alone.

*　　　*　　　*

　　Winter has come with pinching dearth,
　　Lakes all around start to overflow,
　　Frost is crumbling the leaves to earth,
　　Rollicking waves are grumbling low.

*　　　*　　　*

I've heard many times
He won't give horses for poems and rhymes:
He gives what matches his soul anyhow—
A cow.

[OWEN MASTERS]

Summer Is Gone

I have but one story—
The stags are moaning,
The sky is snowing,
Summer is gone.

Quickly the low sun
Goes drifting down
Behind the rollers,
Lifting and long.

The wild geese cry
Down the storm;
The ferns have fallen,
Russet and torn.

The wings of the birds
Are clotted with ice.
I have but one story—
Summer is gone.

[SEAN O'FAOLAIN]

Pangur Ban

I and Pangur Ban my cat
'Tis a like task we are at:
Hunting mice is his delight,
Hunting words I sit all night.

Better far than praise of men
'Tis to sit with book and pen;
Pangur bears me no ill will,
He too plies his simple skill.

'Tis a merry thing to see
At our tasks how glad are we,
When at home we sit and find
Entertainment to our mind.

Oftentimes a mouse will stray
In the hero Pangur's way;
Oftentimes my keen thought set
Takes a meaning in its net.

'Gainst the wall he sets his eye
Full and fierce and sharp and sly;
'Gainst the wall of knowledge I
All my little wisdom try.

When a mouse darts from its den
O how glad is Pangur then!
O what gladness do I prove
When I solve the doubts I love!

So in peace our tasks we ply,
Pangur Ban, my cat and I;
In our arts we find our bliss,
I have mine and he has his.

Practice every day has made
Pangur perfect in his trade;
I get wisdom day and night
Turning darkness into light.

[ROBIN FLOWER]

Fand Yields Cuchulain to Emer

Emer, he is your man, now,
And well may you wear him.
When I can no longer hold him,
I must yield him.

Many a man has wanted me,
But I have kept my vows.
I have been an honest woman,
Under the roofs and boughs.

Pity the woman loves a man,
When no love invites her.
Better for her to fly from love
If unloved, love bites her.

[SEAN O'FAOLAIN]

ANONYMOUS (10th century)

May

May's the merriest time of all,
  Life comes back to everything,
While a ray of light remains
  The never weary blackbirds sing.

That's the cuckoo's strident voice,
  "Welcome summer great and good!"
All the fierceness of the storm
  Lost in tangles of the wood.

Summer stems the languid stream,
  Galloping horses rush the pool,
Bracken bristles everywhere,
  White bog cotton is in bloom.

Scant of breath the burdened bees
  Carry home the flowery spoil,
To the mountains go the cows,
  The ant is glutted with his meal.

The woodland harp plays all day long,
  The sail falls and the world's at rest,
A mist of heat upon the hills
  And the water full of mist.

The corncrake drones, a mighty bard,
  The cold cascade that leaps the rock
Sings of the snugness of the pool,
  Their season come, the rushes talk.

The man grows strong, the virgin blooms
  In all her glory, firm and light,
Bright the far and fertile plain,
  Bright the wood from floor to height.

And here among the meadowlands
　　An eager flock of birds descends,
There a stream runs white and fast
　　Where the murmuring meadow bends.

And you long to race your horse
　　Wildly through the parted crowd,
The sun has scarcely touched the land
　　Yet the waterflags are gold.

Frightened, foolish, frail, a bird
　　Sings of it with throbbing breast,
The lark that flings its praise abroad,
　　May the brightest and the best.

　　　　　　　　　　　　　[FRANK O'CONNOR]

ANONYMOUS (11th century)

Man and Bird and God

What folly for any man on earth
　　His praise of God to end,
When birds don't stop, that have no soul,
　　No spirit, but the wind.

　　　　　　　　　　　　　[OWEN MASTERS]

A Storm At Sea

Tempest on the great seaborders!
Hear my tale, ye viking sworders:
Winter smites us, wild winds crying
Set the salty billows flying,
Wind and winter, fierce marauders.

Ler's vast host of shouting water[1]
Comes against us charged with slaughter;
None can tell the dread and wonder
Speaking in the ocean thunder
And the tempest, thunder's daughter.

With the wind of east at morning
All the waves' wild hearts are yearning
Westward over wastes of ocean
Till they stay their eager motion
Where the setting sun is burning.

When the northern wind comes flying,
All the press of dark waves crying
Southward surge and clamour, driven
To the shining southern heaven,
Wave to wave in song replying.

When the western wind is blowing
O'er the currents wildly flowing,
Eastward sets its mighty longing
And the waves go eastward, thronging
Far to find the sun-tree growing.

When the southern wind comes raining
Over shielded Saxons straining
Waves round Skiddy isle go pouring,
On Caladnet's beaches roaring,
In grey Shannon's mouth complaining.

[1] Manannan macLir (Ler) was the god of the sea.

Full the sea and fierce the surges,
Lovely are the ocean verges,
On the showery waters whirling
Sandy winds are swiftly swirling,
Rudders cleave the surf that urges.

Hard round Eire's cliffs and nesses,
Hard the strife, not soft the stresses,
Like swan-feathers softly sifting
Snow o'er Mile's folk[2] is drifting,
Mannan's wife shakes angry tresses.

At the mouth of each dark river
Breaking waters surge and shiver,
Wind and winter met together
Trouble Alba[3] with wild weather,
Countless falls on Dremon quiver.

Son of God, great Lord of wonder,
Save me from the ravening thunder!
By the feast before Thy dying
Save me from the tempest crying
And from Hell tempestuous under!

[ROBIN FLOWER]

[2] The Irish folk, since Mil was the father of the sixth and last race to invade Ireland.

[3] England.

ANONYMOUS (12th century)

Good Old Finn

If made of gold were brown leaves when
   The forest lets them fall,
If white waves were of silver, Finn
   Would give away them all.

                [OWEN MASTERS]

Crazy Sweeney's Song of the Woods

Antlered being, belling one,
   bleater of musical din,
I love the sound of the stag's cry
   you make deep in the glen.

Homesickness for my dwelling place
   has moved my mind again,
for all the herbs upon the heath,
   the fawns on the mountain fen.

Bushy, leaf-laden tree of oak,
   you tower above each tree;
hazel bush, small branchy one,
   sweet source of nuts for me.

Alder, you are never hostile;
   your hues in beauty glow;
you're not thick with prickly thorns
   in the gully where you grow.

Little blackthorn, thorny one,
  black sloe-bearing thing;
watercress, green-crested one,
  on the brink of blackbird spring.

Tiny thyme along the path,
  sweetest of herbs you seem;
greeny one, greenest of green,
  plant where strawberries teem.

Apple tree, little apple-y one,
  all shake you with much power;
rowan tree, little berried one,
  beautiful is your flower.

Briary bramble, humped in ridges,
  your terms aren't just or good:
you never cease from tearing me
  until you're glutted with blood.

Little yew tree, yewy one,
  in churchyards you abound;
ivy tree, little ivied one,
  in dark woods usually found.

Holly shrub, dark sheltering one,
  a wall to the wind you stand;
tree of ash, baleful one,
  weapon for warrior's hand.

Birchtree, ever blessed and smooth,
  musical, proudly spread,
lovely is every bough entangled
  high on top of your head.

The aspen tree with trembling leaves
  I hear with no delay;
its rustling foliage, quickly racing,
  reminds me of a foray.

If I should roam, forlorn and lone,
   the brown world's mountain chain,
I'd prefer a site for a single hut
   in the Glen of great Bolcain.

An ivy bush, so proud and fine,
   twined through a twisted tree—
if I were on its very tip-top,
   I'd fear from it to flee.

I fly before the flocks of larks—
   a hard and vigorous race;
I leap across the stumps and stalks
   on the mountain's topmost face.

When the proud and plump wood pigeon
   rises for me, high-flown,
I'm quick indeed to overtake it
   since my feathers have grown.

When the silly, clumsy woodcock
   for me begins to rise,
it seems to me an age-old foe,
   and the crow too, with its cries.

Every time I'd make a leap
   and to the ground would go,
I'd surely see the little fox
   gnawing at bones below.

Quicker than wolf among the ivies,
   he'd take advantage of me;
so fast and nimbly would I leap
   that on the peaks I'd be.

Little foxes, full of fraud,
   draw near and run away;
wolves, because of gnashing jaws,
   I flee when I hear them bay.

They tried to catch me very hard,
   approaching swift and sleek,
so that I fled in front of them
   to the top of the mountain peak.

Against me always comes my sin,
   whatever the path I hold;
it's manifest from my laments,
   I'm a sheep without a fold.

The starry frost will come to fall
   and cover every pool;
I'm wretched, wandering on the peaks,
   exposed and pitiful.

The herons with their croaking cry
   in cold Glenelly stay.
A flock of swiftly flying birds
   comes near and goes away.

I do not like the loving talk
   that men and women make;
more musical to me the choiring
   of blackbirds in the brake.

I do not like the trumpeting
   I hear at break of morn;
more musical the squeal of badgers
   on badger mountain born.

I do not like the blowing of horns
   I hear so loud to brag;
more musical the belling call
   of a two-score-antlered stag.

Stag that sends a little sound
   across the glen to me,
good for a lookout post I think
   your antlers' peak would be.

I'm Sweeney, poor old wandering man;
   across the glens I streak;
my name's not right or fit for me;
   best I were called Hornpeak.[1]

Though many have been my wanderings,
   my clothes are scanty now.
My own keen watch I always keep
   atop the mountain's brow.

Bracken, rusty-hued and tall,
   your cloak's been turned to red;
among the branches of your crests
   an outlaw finds no bed.

South, by the strong Taidiu will be
   my last abode of all;
at the abbey of Saint Mo Ling
   by an antler-point I'll fall.

Into your company I am brought
   by the curse of Ronan Finn,
antlered being, belling one,
   bleater of musical din.

[OWEN MASTERS]

---

[1] *Fer Benn*—Man of Peaks, or Antlers.

DONNACHADH MOR O'DALA (*d.* 1244)

At Saint Patrick's Purgatory

Pity me on my pilgrimage to Loch Derg!
O King of the churches and the bells—
Bewailing your sores and your wounds,
But not a tear can I squeeze from my eyes!

Not moisten an eye
After so much sin!
Pity me, O King! What shall I do
With a heart that seeks only its own ease?

Without sorrow or softening in my heart,
Bewailing my faults without repenting them!
Patrick the high priest never thought
That he would reach God in this way.

O lone son of Calpurn—since I name him—
O Virgin Mary, how sad is my lot!—
He was never seen as long as he was in this life
Without the track of tears from his eyes.

In a narrow, hard, stone-walled cell
I lie after all my sinful pride—
O woe, why cannot I weep a tear!—
And I buried alive in the grave.

On the day of Doom we shall weep heavily,
Both the clergy and laity;
The tear that is not dropped in time,
None heeds in the world beyond.

I shall have you go naked, go unfed,
Body of mine, father of sin,
For if you are turned Hellwards
Little shall I reck your agony tonight.

O only begotten Son by whom all men were made,
Who shunned not the death by three wounds,
Pity me on my pilgrimage to Loch Derg
And I with a heart not softer than a stone!

[SEAN O'FAOLAIN]

Old Norse

*U*ntil about 1000 *the Scandinavian countries and Iceland spoke a common North Germanic tongue—Old Norse—but after that date the language began to split into Icelandic, Norwegian and Swedish, with the latter dividing again to add Danish. It is certain that there was an oral tradition of heroic lays, but the existing writing of the pre-Christian era is runic inscriptions, scratched on wood, stone and metal. The history of letters begins with the introduction of Christianity and the adoption of the Latin alphabet.*

The earliest lays were sung in Norway, but after a period of internal conflicts, reflected in the histories and sagas, the center of literature moved to the Norwegian colony of Iceland. This medieval body of work, like the Gaelic, is individual and free of classic Greek-Roman influences, and forms one of the most remarkable of early Germanic literatures. It was set down in books in Iceland. The greatest is the Elder (or Poetic) Edda, *a collection of sagas and lays of the ninth to thirteenth centuries, though the material can be traced to the fourth century.*

The prophecy, "The Beginning and the End", which opens this work, is one of the finest achievements of the period. And the whole work is a major source of the German Nibelungenlied *and Wagner's* Ring *cycle of operas. Because of its length, the poem has unfortunately had to be abridged, as indicated by a series of dots.*

Cormac Ogmundarson and Eyvindr Finsson are examples of the skalds, and may be compared with the Irish and Welsh bards. Skalds were usually attached to the court of a ruler or the household of a chieftain, and their function was to celebrate the feats of their patrons and make poetic records of historical events which could be remembered where the written word was lacking. Eyvindr, in his praise-poem of the hero-king after death, is the type. Cormac, however, is of another sort, since his poems are personal and erotic rather than public and social. All of this poetry is characterized by alliteration and an evocative use of kennings difficult to render in English.

ANONYMOUS (*c.* 900)

The Beginning and The End
A prophetess tells Othin the history of the universe

Hearing I ask from the holy races,
From Heimdall's sons, both high and low;
Thou wilt, Falfather, that well I relate
Old tales I remember of men long ago.

I remember yet the giants of yore,
Who gave me bread in the days gone by;
Nine worlds I knew, the nine in the tree
With mighty roots beneath the mold.

Of old was the age when Ymir lived;
Sea nor cool waves nor sand there were;
Earth had not been, nor heaven above,
But a yawning gap, and grass nowhere.

Then Bur's sons lifted the level land,
Mithgarth the mighty there they made;
The sun from the south warmed the stones of earth,
And green was the ground with growing leeks.

The sun, the sister of the moon, from the south
Her right hand cast over heaven's rim;
No knowledge she had where her home should be,
The moon knew not what might was his,
The stars knew not where their stations were.

Then sought the gods their assembly-seats,
The holy ones, and council held;
Names then gave they to noon and twilight,
Morning they named, and the waning moon,
Night and evening, the years to number.

At Ithavoll met the mighty gods,
Shrines and temples they timbered high;
Forges they set, and they smithied ore,
Tongs they wrought, and tools they fashioned.

In their dwellings at peace they played at tables,
Of gold no lack did the gods then know,—
Till thither came up giant-maids three,
Huge of might out of Jotunheim. . . .

Then from the throng did three come forth,
From the home of the gods, the mighty and gracious;
Two without fate on the land they found,
Ask and Embla, empty of might.

Soul they had not, sense they had not,
Heat nor motion, nor goodly hue;
Soul gave Othin, sense gave Hönir,
Heat gave Lothur and goodly hue.

An ash I know, Yggdrasil its name,
With water white is the great tree wet;
Thence come the dews that fall in the dales,
Green by Urth's well does it ever grow.

Thence come the maidens mighty in wisdom,
Three from the dwelling down 'neath the tree;
Urth is one named, Verthandi the next,—
On the wood they scored,—and Skuld the third.
Laws they made there, and life allotted
To the sons of men, and set their fates.

The war I remember, the first in the world,
When the gods with spears had smitten Gollveig,
And in the hall of Hor had burned her,—
Three times burned, and three times born,
Oft and again, yet ever she lives.

Heith they named her who sought their home,
The wide-seeing witch, in magic wise;
Minds she bewitched that were moved by her magic,
To evil women a joy she was.

On the host his spear did Othin hurl,
Then in the world did war first come;
The wall that girdled the gods was broken,
And the field by the warlike Wanes was trodden.

Then sought the gods their assembly-seats,
The holy ones, and council held,
Whether the gods should tribute give,
Or to all alike should worship belong.

Then sought the gods their assembly-seats,
The holy ones, and council held,
To find who with venom the air had filled,
Or had given Oth's bride to the giants' brood.

In swelling rage then rose up Thor,—
Seldom he sits when he such things hears,—
And the oaths were broken, the words and bonds,
The mighty pledges between them made. . . .

On all sides saw I Valkyries assemble,
Ready to ride to the ranks of the gods;
Skuld bore the shield, and Skogul rode next,
Guth, Hild, Gondul, and Geirskogul.
Of Herjan's maidens the list have ye heard,
Valkyries ready to ride o'er the earth.

I saw for Baldr, the bleeding god,
The son of Othin, his destiny set:
Famous and fair in the lofty fields,
Full grown in strength the mistletoe stood.

From the branch which seemed so slender and fair
Came a harmful shaft that Hoth should hurl;
But the brother of Baldr was born ere long,
And one night old fought Othin's son.

His hands he washed not, his hair he combed not,
Till he bore to the bale-blaze Baldr's foe,
But in Fensalir did Frigg weep sore
For Valhall's need: would you know yet more?

One did I see in the wet woods bound,
A lover of ill, and to Loki like;
By his side does Sigyn sit, nor is glad
To see her mate: would you know yet more? . . . .

The giantess old in Ironwood sat,
In the east, and bore the brood of Fenrir;
Among these one in monster's guise
Was soon to steal the sun from the sky.

There feeds he full on the flesh of the dead,
And the home of the gods he reddens with gore;
Dark grows the sun, and in summer soon
Come mighty storms: would you know yet more?

On a hill there sat, and smote on his harp,
Eggther the joyous, the giants' warder;
Above him the cock in the bird-wood crowed,
Fair and red did Fjalar stand.

Then to the gods crowed Gollinkambi,
He wakes the heroes in Othin's hall;
And beneath the earth does another crow,
The rust-red birds at the bars of Hel.

Now Garm howls loud before Gnipahellir,
The fetters will burst, and the wolf run free;
Much do I know, and more can see
Of the fate of the gods, the mighty in fight.

Brothers shall fight and fell each other,
And sisters' sons shall kinship stain;
Hard is it on earth, with mighty whoredom;
Ax-time, sword-time, shields are sundered,
Wind-time, wolf-time, ere the world falls;
Nor ever shall men each other spare.

Fast move the sons of Mim, and fate
Is hard in the note of the Ghallarhorn;
Loud blows Heimdall, the horn is aloft,
In fear quake all who on Hel-roads are.

Yggdrasil shakes, and shiver on high
The ancient limbs, and the giant is loose;
To the head of Mim does Othin give heed,
But the kinsman of Surt shall slay him soon.

How fare the gods? how fare the elves?
All Jotunheim groans, the gods are at council;
Loud roar the dwarfs by the doors of stone,
The masters of the rocks: would you know yet more?

Now Garm howls loud before Gnipahellir,
The fetters will burst, and the wolf run free;
Much do I know, and more can see
Of the fate of the gods, the mighty in fight.

From the east comes Hrym with shield held high;
In giant-wrath does the serpent writhe;
O'er the waves he twists, and the tawny eagle
Gnaws corpses screaming; Naglfar is loose.

O'er the sea from the north there sails a ship
With the people of Hel, at the helm stands Loki;
After the wolf do wild men follow,
And with them the brother of Byleist goes.

Surt fares from the south with the scourge of branches,
The sun of the battle-gods shone from his sword;
The crags are sundered, the giant-women sink,
The dead throng Hel-way, and heaven is cloven.

Now comes to Hlin yet another hurt,
When Othin fares to fight with the wolf,
And Beli's fair slayer seeks out Surt,
For there must fall the joy of Frigg.

Then comes Sigfather's mighty son,
Vithar, to fight with the foaming wolf;
In the giant's son does he thrust his sword
Full to the heart: his father is avenged.

Hither there comes the son of Hlothyn,
The bright snake gapes to heaven above;
.   .   .   .
Against the serpent goes Othin's son.

In anger smites the warder of earth,—
Forth from their homes must all men flee;—
Nine paces fares the son of Fjorgyn,
And, slain by the serpent, fearless he sinks.

The sun turns black, earth sinks in the sea,
The hot stars down from heaven are whirled;
Fierce grows the steam and the life-feeding flame,
Till fire leaps high above heaven itself.

Now Garm howls loud before Gnipahellir,
The fetters will burst, and the wolf run free;
Much do I know, and more can see
Of the fate of the gods, the mighty in fight.

Now do I see the earth anew
Rise all green from the waves again;
The cataracts fall, and the eagle flies,
And fish he catches beneath the cliffs.

The gods in Ithavoll meet together,
Of the terrible girdler of earth they talk,
And the mighty past they call to mind,
And the ancient runes of the Ruler of Gods.

In wondrous beauty once again
Shall the golden tables stand mid the grass,
Which the gods had owned in the days of old. . . .

Then fields unsowed bear ripened fruit,
All ills grow better, and Baldr comes back;
Baldr and Hoth dwell in Hropt's battle-hall,
And the mighty gods: would you know yet more? . . . .

More fair than the sun, a hall I see,
Roofed with gold, on Gimle it stands;
There shall the righteous rulers dwell,
And happiness ever there shall they have. . . .

From below the dragon dark comes forth,
Nithhogg flying from Nithalfjoll;
The bodies of men on his wings he bears,
The serpent bright: but now must I sink.

[HENRY ADAMS BELLOWS]

CORMAC OGMUNDARSON (*c.* 930–970)

Three Songs to Steingerd

1.

There breaks on me, burning upon me,
A blaze from the cheeks of a maiden,
—I laugh not to look on the vision—
In the light of the hall by the doorway.
So sweet and so slender I deem her,
Though I spy but a glimpse of an ankle
By the threshold:—and through me there flashes
A thrill that shall age never more.

2.

Yea, black are the eyes that I bring ye,
O brave in your jewels, and dainty.
But a draggle-tail, dirty-foot slattern
Would dub me ill-favored and sallow.
Nay, many a maiden has loved me,
Thou may of the glittering armlet:
For I've tricks of the tongue to beguile them
And turn them from handsome lads.

3.

The tree of my treasure and longing,
It would take this whole Iceland to win her:
She is dearer than far-away Denmark,
And the doughty domain of the Hun-folk.
With the gold she is combing, I count her
More costly than England could ransom:
So witty, so wealthy, my lady
Is worth them,—and Ireland beside!

[W. G. COLLINGWOOD AND JON STEFANSSON]

EYVINDR FINSSON (10th century)

Death Song of Haakon the Good

Gondul and Skogul   the great god sent
    To choose from the kings
Of the race of Yngvi   the one to join Odin
    And dwell in Valhalla.

They found Bjorn's brother   donning his buckler;
The staunch noble king   by his standard stood.
Shafts of death showered   and darts shot quivering.
    The battle was broached.

The liege men of Roga   and Haloga were roused
By the slayer of earls   as he strode to battle.
The prince, well-supported   by proud Norse bands,
The dread of the Danes,   in bright helmet was dressed.

Leading choice legions,   he laid off his war-gear,
And flung down his mail-coat   before he would fight.
In gold helmet, gleaming,   as guard for the land,
With the soldiers he stood   and joyously sported.

From the sea-king's hand   the sword cut the robes
Of Odin, as the weapons   smote through the water.
Spearheads were shivered   and shields were shattered,
Steel struck and clanged   on the skulls of warriors.

Crushed were the breastplates   and skulls by the blade
Of the generous monarch   of the men of the North,
In the rout on the island   where the kings made red
The bulwark of shields   with the blood of soldiers.

And sword-fire blazed   in the bleeding wounds,
And pole-axes leaned   to let men's lives.
On blades gushed blood-surf   like breakers on rocks;
Gore rolled in a sea   on the shores of Stord.

The spear-surge heaved   in the sky of red shields,
As Skogul billowed   storm clouds around bucklers.
Red waves of blood   in Odin's gale roared.
Overthrown were throngs   by the thick tide of blades.

Now the princes were sitting,   drawn swords at their sides,
With shields all cloven   and mail-coats pierced.
Not happy in heart   was the army that took
        Its way to Valhalla.

Then Gondul spoke—   she grasped her spear-shaft—
        "The gods' host grows,
Now that Haakon is bidden   with so great a band
        To their hallowed homes."

The king understood   the Valkyries' speech.
        Solemn and poised,
They bestrode their horses,   with helmeted heads
        And shields held firm.

"Why have you fated   the fray thus, Skogul?
    We surely were worthy   of winning the battle!"
"We have willed it so   that you've won," said Skogul,
        "Your foes have fallen."

"With Gondul I ride,"   said radiant Skogul,
        "To the green world of gods,
To announce to Odin   that a new king hastens
        To stand before him."

"Hermod and Bragi,"   said Odin almighty,
        "Go meet this monarch,
For a prince who is proven   a hero approaches
        Our hall of the slain."

Then spake the prince,   come fresh from fighting,
        Still bathed in blood:
"Most hostile to us   has Odin behaved.
        His face shows disfavor."

"From none of the heroes   shall you know any harm.
              Drink ale with the Aesir!
Oh enemy of earls,   you have in our home
              Eight brothers," said Bragi.

"Close in our keeping,"   said the brave king,
              "We will hold our armor;
Weapons and helms   must be well-watched;
              It's good to have gear by."

It was plainly shown   how the king had paid
              Respect to the shrines,
When Haakon was hailed   by the council of gods
              With a welcome of warmth.

A prince who attains   such noble distinction
              Was born in good luck.
His life will ever   be lauded and held
              Full of glory and honor.

On the world, man's home,   will be loosed for woe,
              The fierce wolf, Fenrir,
Before there follows   on his empty throne
              So peerless a prince.

Estates are drained off,   kinsmen are dying,
              The land is laid waste;
Since Haakon went far   to the heathen gods,
              Many to bondage are brought.

[O. L. OLIVER]

Danish

Danish is closely related to the Swedish branch of the three languages that evolved from Old Norse. The earliest literature of Denmark, as of other Scandinavian countries, is runic—brief epitaphs, often in alliterative verse, incised on stone. With the advent of Christianity, which meant also the advent of Latin, Danish writers of prose and poetry started composing in Latin.

Works in the vernacular, such as local and church laws, medical books, hymns, collections of proverbs, appeared in the twelfth century, and from this period the earliest ballads also date. Though many literatures have brief narrative poems in a style suggesting that they are prototypes of the ballad—which they may indeed be—the true major characteristics of the ballad are absent.

The Danish ballads precede those of all other countries, and for that reason I give a few specimens here and omit the form from the other language groups except the Spanish (where they are called "romances"). It might be well to note, however, that the ballad in Sweden arose about this time (but few were transcribed until the *nineteenth century); and in Russia in the thirteenth century, in Spain, Scotland and England in the fourteenth, in Germany in the fifteenth.*

These anonymous poems are the finest literature of medieval Denmark, and nearly all were written down by the end of the Middle Ages. The first printed edition was published in 1591. In all, 539 distinct ballads are known in over 3000 versions.

ANONYMOUS BALLADS

The Elected Knight

Sir Oluf he rideth over the plain,
   Full seven miles broad and seven miles wide;
But never, ah! never, can meet with the man
   A tilt with him dare ride.

He saw under the hill-side
   A knight full well equipped;
His steel was black, his helm was barred;
   He was riding at full speed.

He wore upon his spurs
   Twelve little golden birds;
Anon in eddies the wild wind blew,
   And there sat all the birds and sang.

He wore upon his mail
   Twelve little golden wheels;
Anon in eddies the wild wind blew,
   And round and round the wheels they flew.

He wore before his breast
　A lance that was poised in rest,
And it was sharper than diamond-stone;
　It made Sir Oluf's heart to groan.

He wore upon his helm
　A wreath of ruddy gold;
And that gave him the Maidens Three,
　The youngest was fair to behold.

Sir Oluf questioned the knight eftsoon
　If he were come from heaven down;
"Art thou Christ of Heaven?" quoth he,
　"So will I yield me unto thee."

"I am not Christ the Great,
　Thou shalt not yield thee yet;
I am an Unknown Knight,
　Three modest Maidens have me bedight."

"Art thou a knight elected?
　And have three maidens thee bedight?
So shalt thou ride a tilt this day,
　For all the maidens' honor!"

The first tilt they together rode,
　They put their steeds to the test;
The second tilt they together rode,
　They proved their manhood best.

The third tilt they together rode,
　Neither of them would yield;
The fourth tilt they together rode,
　They both fell on the field.

Now lie the lords upon the plain,
　And their blood runs unto death;
Now sit the Maidens in the high tower,
　The youngest sorrows till death.

[H. W. LONGFELLOW]

The Avenging Daughters

Sister to sister said:
(For him who loveth me)
"Wouldst thou not fain be wed?"
She dwelleth under greenwood tree.

"None will I wed while I draw breath
Till I avenge my father's death."

"Thou speak'st an idle word,
We have neither mail nor sword."

"Here are rich franklins dwelling in town,
Swords will they lend us and byrnies brown."

When they came to Rose-bower
They met Sir Erlend that selfsame hour.

"Sure, ye twain are bridegrooms bold,
A-riding forth some tryst to hold!"

"Now nay, we are not bridegrooms bold,
But truly we ride a tryst to hold."

"I rede ye ride by wood and wold
To two fair orphans with store of gold."

"If they have store of pelf
Why dost not woo thyself?"

"I would flee them rather
For I have slain their father,

"And I have slain their brother,
And I have beguiled their mother."

"Yea, thou hast slain father and brother,
But thou liest concerning our mother!"

So womanlike their swords they drew,
So manlike did they hack and hew.

They hewed Sir Erlend to pieces small
As the leaves that under the linden fall.

Sorely the maidens wept for dread
When to shrive their souls they sped.

All the penance they got for Sir Erlend's slaughter
Was Fridays three on bread and water.

[E. M. SMITH-DAMPIER]

The Maiden Hind

The mother to her son did say:
(In the greenwood)
"The little hind thou shalt not slay,
That bears the band of gold.

"Mayst slay the hart and shoot the doe,
But the little hind must thou let go."

Sir Peter rode in greenwood bound,
And the little hind played before his hound.

The little hind sported his feet before,
And he thought on his mother's words no more.

He spanned his crossbow with hand and knee,
And shot the hind beside a tree.

His gloves from off his hands he drew
To flay the hind without ado.

Her neck he flayed, and there
Was his sister's golden hair.

He found in her bosom cold
His sister's rings of gold.

In her side with sore affright
He found her hands so white.

His hunting-knife to the ground he threw:
"Now has my mother's tale come true!"

Cold on the river falleth the rime,
There is luck for the lad who can take it in time.

Far the crane flieth up in the sky.
Lucky the lad who from trouble can fly!

[E. M. SMITH-DAMPIER]

Aager and Eliza

'Twas the valiant knight, Sir Aager,
  He to the far island hied,
There he wedded sweet Eliza,
  She of maidens was the pride.

There he married sweet Eliza,
  With her lands and ruddy gold;
Woe is me! the Monday after,
  Dead he lay beneath the mould.

In her bower sat sweet Eliza,
  Screamed, and would not be consoled;
And the good Sir Aager listened,
  Underneath the dingy mould.

Up Sir Aager rose, his coffin
  Bore he on his bended back:
Towards the bower of sweet Eliza
  Was his sad and silent track.

He the door tapped with his coffin,
  For his fingers had no skin:
"Rise, O, rise, my sweet Eliza!
  Rise, and let thy bridegroom in."

Straightway answered fair Eliza:
  "I will not undo my door,
Till thou name the name of Jesus,
  Even as thou could'st before."

"Rise, O, rise, mine own Eliza,
  And undo thy chamber door!
I can name the name of Jesus,
  Even as I could of yore."

Up then rose the sweet Eliza,
  Down her cheeks tears streaming ran;
Unto her within the bower
  She admits the spectre man.

She her golden comb has taken,
  And has combed his yellow hair.
On each lock that she adjusted
  Fell a hot and briny tear.

"Listen now, my good Sir Aager!
  Dearest bridegroom, all I crave
Is to know how goes it with thee
  In that lonely place, the grave?"

"Every time that thou rejoicest,
  And art happy in thy mind,
Are my lonely grave's recesses
  All with leaves of roses lined.

"Every time that, love, thou grievest,
  And dost shed the briny flood,
Are my lonely grave's recesses
  Filled with black and loathesome blood.

"Heard I not the red cock crowing?
  I, my dearest, must away;
Down to earth the dead are going,
  And behind I must not stay.

"Heard I not the black cock crowing?
  To the grave I down must go;
Now the gates of heaven are opening,
  Fare thee well for ever more."

Up Sir Aager stood, the coffin
  Takes he on his bended back;
To the dark and distant church-yard
  Is his melancholy track.

Up then rose the sweet Eliza,
  Full courageous was her mood;
And her bridegroom she attended
  Through the dark and dreary wood.

When the forest they had traversed,
  And within the church-yard were,
Faded then of good Sir Aager
  Straight the lovely yellow hair.

When the church-yard they had traversed
  And the church's threshold crossed,
Straight the cheek of good Sir Aager
  All its rosy color lost.

"Listen now, my sweet Eliza!
  If my peace be dear to thee,
Never thou, from this time forward,
  Pine or shed a tear for me.

"Turn, I pray thee, up to heaven
  To the little stars thy sight:
Then thou mayest know for certain
  How it fareth with the knight."

Soon as e'er her eyes to heaven
  To the little stars she reared,
Into earth the dead man glided,
  And to her no more appeared.

Homeward went the sweet Eliza.
  Grief of her had taken hold;
Woe is me! the Monday after,
  Dead she lay beneath the mould.

                              [ANONYMOUS TRANSLATOR]

Dutch

In the Dark Ages several tribes speaking dialects of West Germanic languages inhabited what are now Germany and The Netherlands. Old Low German, spoken by the Franks, Frisians and Saxons, evolved into modern Dutch and Flemish, Old High German into the modern German. A literature of heroic lays existed in Frankish, and was later enlarged by borrowed or translated romances and epics of chivalry.

Though a vernacular literature had begun in the twelfth century, it was not until the mid-thirteenth that a genuine Dutch poetic literature emerged. The earliest known poet, Heinrich von Veldeke (fl. 1170–90), wrote some slight lyrics in the Limburg dialect. It has been assumed that Troubadours must have visited some of the ruling courts and influenced the native poets; but if so, the Dutch troubadour poems are lost.

However, without this hypothesis, it is difficult to account for the sudden appearance and quality of the poems by the nun, Hadewijch, about 1250. Though her work is ecstatic and mystical, proclaiming a love of God, the style and form are plainly troubadour. And strangely enough, she is the only Dutch poet, until the Renaissance, who can interest modern readers other than scholars. Similarities to later mystical poets (St. Teresa, St. John of the Cross, S. Marcela de Carpio, etc.) in the often embarassingly sensual expression of heavenly love, probably springs from the nature of religious ecstasy and Biblical symbolism, rather than from her literary influence.

HADEWIJCH (13th century)

The Eighteenth Song

The new year hath come in sight,
Now to God our blessings bring!
He who findeth in Love delight,
Joyfully will hail the spring.
And he who in his heart is aware
That for high love he will care
Will ever gladly be suffering.

He who shall serve in love's array
Must ever be a sufferer,
And heighten in love his service ay,
If he shall have reward from her
And rise to that nature high above
In the which love loveth with love,
Who stole his heart and character.

From new delight and love there grew
For both, in one ground, pains that smart.
That I know it again for new
Maketh a wound now in my heart:
That the figure so noble and strong
Was concealed from us so long
And set in her subtle nature apart.

To him who served in love anew
It would seem a hard ordeal.
For one now findeth very few
Who care to taste true love's appeal.
To cruel strangers remaineth concealed
How my heart would never yield
To me the joy I long to feel.

[A. J. BARNOUW]

The Nineteenth Song

Great good fortune ere it is had
And great promise before the pay
Should not make any person glad.
Little of both has come my way.
  Love's early sign
  Before she was mine
Has driven me out of me, weilaway!

At the promise of the dawn's red
One hopeth for the light clear day.
By glimmers of love I was misled,
And many others I won't betray.
  They know themselves who were.
  I'm one who can declare
That I have never yet by love been sped.

The churl he saith, "Toward evening
One ought to praise the bonny day."
Because too late I learnt such thing
I now may cry, "O Weilaway!"
  Where is that solace now
  With the peace with which thou,
O love, first seemed to come my way?

She seemed to show me naught but good
And then turned cruel. Yet now I know
She didn't, as I misunderstood,
Deceive me with a feignëd show.
      She meant to make me see
      That reason wonderfully
Illumes the deepest ground of love through woe.

Illumined reason, in company
With highest love, they will permit
To inspect with her love's garden and see
If there's enough of all in it.
      Is there a lack,
      Do not be slack:
Supply it, with deeds that love befit.

O were my faith so strong withal
That love had no reproach for me,
And would repay all mine with all,
That I be counted such as I be!
      First I would ask,
      Then call to task
Love for remissness candidly.

O noble love, what time, O when
Wilt thou give me sunlit days,
So that my darkness shall be spent?
I wish I saw the sun's bright rays!
      Thou knowest alone
      Whereto I am prone,
If I want aught but what thee please.

Thou wieldest power, love, wondrously,
And wondrously canst all o'erpower.
O vanquish me, that I vanquish thee,
In thine ever unvanquished dower.
    I used to know this vanquishing,
    Which made of me a wiser thing,
Through knowledge such as made me cower.

Thou still art what thou ever wert.
They know who are with thee in all.
From praise of thee I shan't revert.
Only a mishap made me stall:
    That I perceived not yet
    Nor loved the travail that
Was meant to make me ready for the call.

Since I have walked in high belief
That love would be my aid and stay,
I left behind all alien grief
And stood in hope from day to day,
    In which I'm sure
    Love will immure
Me with her all in every way.

Of high love's way this much I know:
She downs the lover under her stroke,
And yet, o'erpowered and beaten low,
Sweet and sufficient he finds the yoke.
    Hence of her ways
    High laud and praise
Throughout the land they ever spoke.

Love seizes one and closes his eyes
With pleasures; he thinks all his is best!
And fancies tasting naught but joys.
Thus draws she all with lusty zest.
    Then reason, the strong,
    Brings new travail along
Of guilt. Thus is the fire repressed.

Many a song of love I've sung.
But it booted me little and did me no good.
Yet every one, the old and the young,
Through songs of love feel cooled in mood.
    But my whole has but small
    Part of love's all:
My song, my crying in vain intrude.

    My plaint I raise:
    Love has the days,
And I the nights and love's hardihood.

        [A. J. BARNOUW]

German

Not much German poetry, especially lyric, has come down to us from the years before the full development of the Minnesingers in the later half of the twelfth century. There are fragments of several ninth century heroic poems in alliterative verse and a few lyrics in rhyme from later dates. The love songs of Dietmar von Aist and the Knight of Kürenberg, in which usually a lady tells of her longing for her knight (such poems are called Frauenstrophen), seem to spring naturally from the culture of chivalry.

With the first flowering of the Minnesingers in Friedrich von Hausen, the address of the poems changed: the knight now generally longs for his lady. The style and temperament derive from the Provençal Troubadours, having spread through France and the Low Countries; but already Dietmar, probably familiar with their songs, had written the Dawn-song (Tagelied) given below.

Most of the later poets followed the convention of adoration of an unapproachable, preferably married, noblewoman, and sought to rationalize their paradoxical situation by praising the "ennobling *effects of hopeless love". It is much the same attitude that many of the Italian poets took, though it is apparent in all the literatures influenced by the Troubadours.*

At length the convention began to chafe the poets. Walther von der Vogelweide and Wolfram von Eschenbach dealt with genuine emotions and demanded that love be requited. In fact, Walther went so far as to flout the courtly ideal and choose a village girl as his "lady". Within 150 years, the original force of the chivalric lyrics had exhausted itself, and the last Minnesingers, such as Reinmar von Sweter and Neidhart von Reuenthal, turned to parody of the earlier songs, as well as to satires of both chivalry and peasantry. Finally the brightness of the Minnesinger lyrics died out under the suffocating pall of the Meistersingers.

ANONYMOUS (12th century)

Reward of Service

"A knight there is," a lady said,
"Hath served me as I wished full fain.
Or ere the time of year be fled,
His due reward he needs must gain.
Now snow and winter seem to me
Flowers and clover fair to be,
When in my arms I hold him fast.
Though all the world should take it ill,
Yet must he get his will at last!"

[F. C. NICHOLSON]

DIETMAR VON AIST (*fl.* 1140–70)

The Linden Tree

There sat upon the linden tree
  A bird and sang its strain;
So sweet it sang, that, as I heard,
  My heart went back again:
It went to one remembered spot,
  I saw the rose-trees grow,
And thought again the thoughts of love
  There cherished long ago.

A thousand years to me it seems
  Since by my fair I sat,
Yet thus to have been stranger long
  Was not my choice, but fate:
Since then I have not seen the flowers,
  Nor heard the birds' sweet song;
My joys have all too briefly passed,
  My griefs been all too long.

[EDGAR TAYLOR]

Dawn Song

"Oh handsome love, are you still asleep?
We'd soon be waked by chirp and peep:
A little bird, so fine to see,
Has perched upon a branch of the linden tree."

"I'd fallen asleep in peace till dawn.
Now you call, darling, awake, begone.
No love can be without some dismay.
My sweet, I'll do whatever thing you say."

The lady began to weep and moan.
"Far off you'll ride, and leave me alone.
When will you come again in view?
Alas, you'll take my joy away with you."

[O. L. OLIVER]

THE KNIGHT OF KÜRENBERG (*c.* 1150–70)

The Falcon

I raised a noble falcon
For more than a year;
And when I had tamed him
And decked his feathers, tying
Them with a golden band,
He rose so swiftly, flying
Far to another land.
Since then I've seen my falcon
Gaily soaring;
And from his feet were waving
Fair silken ribbons,
And on his wings each feather
Was ruddy gold to see;
Ah, God bring those together
Who lovers fain would be!

[MARGARETE MÜNSTERBERG]

Star

The star darkly gleaming   hides its dim light.
So do thou, fair lady,   when I stand in thy sight,
Then let thine eyes rest   upon some other man.
Then none shall guess easily   what we two there may plan.

[MARGARET R. RICHEY]

FRIEDRICH VON HAUSEN (*fl.* 1170–90)

Civil War

My heart and body would fain part company,
Who have fared together for a long time past.
My body would fight the Paynim oversea,
But my heart on a lady fixed fast
Its choice, and now in trouble I am cast,
Sore grieving that those twain asunder flee.
Mine eyes have wrought much mischief unto me.
Now may God end this struggle at the last!

    I looked to be released from all my woe,
When once I took the Cross in Heaven's name.
And well might it have happened even so,
Were not my constancy itself to blame.
I should be whole and sound, quit of this shame,
Would but my heart its fond desire forgo;
But little recks it now, too well I know,
What fortune may befall me in the game.

    Since o'er thee, heart of mine, I have no might,
But thou wilt surely go and let me grieve,
I pray to God that He direct thy flight
Where thou a gracious welcome shalt receive.
Alas, what will betide thee? Darest thou leave,
Against such troubles all alone to fight?
For who like me will help thee 'scape despite,
Who cleave to thee as I was wont to cleave?

[F. C. NICHOLSON]

HARTMANN VON AUE (*c.* 1170–1215)

The Scales of Love

Were I to hate the one who injures me,
I am my foe, and must myself malign.
Of fickleness, it seems, I am not free:
My sorrow is of this the outward sign.
My lady loves me not, the fault is mine.
Since sense brings joy, as is all men's belief,
And lack of sense is granted no relief
In love, then was my love a fool's in brief,
And I alone am guilty of my grief.

Since she was right my homage to despise,
If she her noble body did protect
From my complaints and passion, she was wise.
Thus was my anger lacking in respect,
And hath but aged me. Seeing my defect,
She shunned me, cruelly deliberate
But justly; and I praise her for her hate,
And for her honor she would not abate
To succour one whose faults deserved his fate.

She judged at random, nor as I deserved,
When first she took my oath and fealty:
But when she saw my service sank and swerved,
My frail love and her logic ruined me.
Yet hath she granted what she promised; she
Seeks not the debt she owes me to retain:
She weighed me in the scales, and fixed love's gain
To the measure of the merest dram and grain.
Thus reason shows: by my own sword I'm slain.

[JETHRO BITHELL]

HEINRICH VON MORUNGEN (d. 1222)

Two Remember Dawn

Alas! shall ever I see again,
Gleaming athwart the night,
Whiter than driven snow,
Her body bright?
Thus were my eyes deceived,
For I believed
It was the moon's clear ray
That shone.
Suddenly day
Broke, and the night was gone.

"Alas! and will he ever again
Be here when the dawn turns gray,
So that we need not rue
The approach of day—
As when he made lament
The last night he spent
Lying by the side of me.
Anon
Day suddenly
Broke, and the night was gone."

Alas! she kissed me in my sleep
Times beyond all telling.
Her cheek was wet with tears
From her eyes welling.
Gently I bade her cease,
And she, at peace,
Her arms about me, lay
Held fast.
Suddenly day
Broke, and the night was past.

"Alas! how often has he stayed
His wondering gaze on me!
My white arms he unbared
So lovingly.
It was a deep surprise
That his rapt eyes
He could not draw away.
At last,
Too soon, the day
Broke, and the night was past."

[MARGARET R. RICHEY]

Song

Hast thou seen
My heart's true queen
At the window gazing;
Her whose love
Can care remove,
All my sorrows easing?
Like the sun at first uprising,
She was shrouded;
And o'erclouded
Was my spirit,—now rejoicing.

Is there none
Whose heart can own
A generous, kindly feeling?
Let him aid me
Find that lady
Who from me is stealing;
That her beauteous smile may cheer me
Ere I go;
For love and woe
To the silent grave fast bear me.

Then upon
My burial-stone
Men shall write how dearly
She was prized,
And I despised,
I that loved sincerely;
Then the passing swain shall see
My complaining,
Her disdaining;
Such sad fate she dealt to me.

[EDGAR TAYLOR]

Dream and Image

Troubles, they say, are sent us to grow wise on.
Even as a child sees its sweet image lined
Within a glass, grasps at it, and then cries on
The shattered fragments, in my wiser mind
Love so lies bleeding sad and unresigned.
The zenith blue that, when I first set eyes on
My lady, domed a distant, dark horizon,
Is gone, and has not left a gleam behind.

    Love, to my cries of passion half replying,
Dreamwise brought to my couch my fancies' queen!
And, though with sleep-bound arms and senses sighing,
I lay and looked, and saw her to demean
The soothing sweetness of her beauties' sheen,
All other ladies' beauty far out-vieing:
Save that her mouth was hurt, and thereon lying
The shadow of a sorrow dimly seen.

    Now, after that frail vision dream-detected,
I fear lest her red lips grow pale and dim;
And must henceforth be ever deep dejected,
That these poor eyes of mine should dare to limn,
Though innocent in sleep, such ruin grim:
Even as a foolish youth that, unsuspected,
Comes on his shadow in a well reflected,
And loves it until death releases him.

[JETHRO BITHELL]

REINMAR VON HAGENAU (*fl.* 1190–1210)

Deduction

One thing they say displeases me:
Indeed, it almost puts me in a rage.
They keep on asking me my lady's age,
And want to know, how old is she,
Because I have been serving her so long,
They say it to incense me.
May the sweet mistress of my song
For that ill-mannered question recompense me!

[MARGARET R. RICHEY]

A Meadow and My Lady

I saw the meadow sweetly set
With many a flower red and bright.
Full lovely is the violet;
The nightingale hath conquered quite
The sore distress that did her wrong.
Now vanished is the winter long:
I have heard her song!
    I cast away the care I felt,
When first the green leaves I did see.
Toward me a lady so hath dealt
That evermore my heart must be
Filled full of rapture and delight.
Whate'er she do from morn to night,
I'll deem it right.

My sorrow she hath all removed,
So that no more I pine and ail.
Four thousand ladies would have proved,
Without her help, of no avail.
Her kindness drives my grief away,
And her true love I am today,
Whate'er folk say.

Henceforth I shall not fear at all
That I may meet with any harm.
Were what I long for to befall,
She soon should lie within my arm.
Her beauty's prize I should obtain;
'Twere sweet, methinks, and I were fain
Such bliss to gain.

That toward her so my heart is bent
Vexes and angers not a few.
I'll never fear their discontent;
They lose their toil whate'er they do.
What profits all their scheming base?
They know not what hath taken place
In this brief space!

[F. C. NICHOLSON]

WOLFRAM VON ESCHENBACH (*fl.* 1200–20)

Hope For Miracles

A lady may allow me be so bold
To mark her beauty as my passion would.
I wish—and shall do even if she scold—
To let my eyes dwell in her neighborhood.
How comes it that I am an owl in sight?
My heart can see her in the depths of night.
    What injury does a stork unto the corn?
Less injury the ladies have of me.
Their hatred would be cruel to be borne:
But I deserve it not; and hope to see
A day that sees me at the height of bliss.
Still greater wonders have occurred ere this.

[JETHRO BITHELL]

WALTER VON DER VOGELWEIDE (1170–1228)

Blessed Be the Hour

Blessed be the hour when first I knew her,
Her who with heart and soul did rout me;
When all my senses were aroused to woo her,
I felt her goodness hover all about me.
And now I cannot part from her again,
Because her beauty and kindness delight me,
And her red, red mouth that laughs so brightly.

My heart and mind I have been turning
Unto the pure one, the good one, the dear one.
Ah, could I but fulfill my yearning:
I trust to her mercy that she will hear one.
All my joy on earth doth come from her,
Because her beauty and kindness delight me,
And her red, red, mouth that laughs so brightly.

[MARGARETE MÜNSTERBERG]

The Oracle

Beset with doubts, in agony
I sat quite long alone and thought
How from her service I might be free,
Until a comfort gladness brought.
This thing a comfort I can hardly call,
'Tis scarce a baby comfort—oh, so small!
And if I tell you, you'll be mocking me:
Yet without cause no one can happy be.

A little stalk has made me glad today;
It promised happiness I never knew:
I measured with a stalk of straw in play,
As I had often seen the children do.
Now listen, if her heart my love has heeded:
"She loves—loves not—she loves!" Which way my
                              hands would bend,
"She loves me!" always was the end.
So I am happy; only—faith is needed.

[MARGARETE MÜNSTERBERG]

For One of Low Degree

Sweetheart, young mistress mine,
God bless thee this and every day:
Could I some wish define
Greater than this, for thee, I'd pray
For words to utter it; what can I say more
Than this, that no one cares for thee as I do: whence my heart
is sore.

They tell me, I do ill to address
My song to one of low degree;
But they reveal their wit the less,
Who thus disclaim what love should be.
Let us not heed their jibes, they do not know
Love's meaning, they who are in love with wealth and with
fair outward show.

Beauty tends to cruelty:
Of Beauty's wiles let all beware.
Love can fill the heart with glee:
Beauty with Love may not compare.
Love makes a woman beauteous to behold.
Beauty has not the gift to make her lovable, if truth be told.

As I have borne, so let me bear,
And still continue to endure.
Thy fortune and thy face are fair,
Let no one speak of thee as poor!
Whate'er they say, I love thee in such measure,
The ring of glass thou gavest me would I not change for a
queen's treasure.

If thy heart be leal and true,
I shall not suffer doubt, nor dread
Lest thou shouldst give me cause to rue
My love, and wish its vows unsaid.
If it be otherwise, then let us go
Our separate ways alone; but ah, what pain, if that were
                                        really so!
                              [MARGARET R. RICHEY]

Under the Linden

Under the linden by the heather
There was prepared for two our bed,
There you may find so fair together
Gathered flowers and grasses spread.
Off by the forest in the dale,
                    Tandaradei!
Sweetly sang the nightingale.

I to the field came for our meeting.
There my dear love had come before.
He called me Noble Lady in greeting,
Which will delight me evermore.
Kisses, you ask? A thousand, I vow,
                    Tandaradei!
See how red my lips are now!

He had arranged a bed so splendid,
Fashioned of flowers white and pink.
Anyone who that path descended
Warmly would smile to himself, I think:
From the rose-petals all too plain,
                    Tandaradei!
He'll see where my head has lain.

If it were known (God grant it's never)
He lay with me, how shamed I'd be!
Just what he did, may no one ever
Know except only him and me,
And a tiny little bird as well,
                    Tandaradei!
But we trust it never to tell.

[O. L. OLIVER]

REINMAR VON SWETER (*fl.* 1227–47)

Fortitude

Sir Cock, to you the first place I award
In bravery's annals, for you are the lord
And master of your wives, although you have so many.
Now for my sins God gave but one to me,
But she has robbed me of my sanity,
And all the joy she leaves me is not worth a penny.
Had I two such I should not dare to laugh,
Four and I would prepare mine epitaph,
Eight and the sexton straight my grave should delve.
I should be torn in shreds within an hour!
Sir Cock, thank God that he has given you power,
For your good luck to master even twelve.

[JETHRO BITHELL]

NEIDHART VON REUENTHAL (*c.* 1180–*c.* 1250)

On the Mountain

On the mountain, in the valley,
Singing birds again do rally;
Now is seen
Clover green;
Winter, take away thy teen!
Trees that erst were gray to view
Now their verdant robes renew;
In their shade
Nests are made;
Thence the toll of May is paid.
Fought an aged wife for breath
Day and night, and baffled death;
Now she rushes
Like a ram about, and pushes
All the young ones into the bushes.

[JETHRO BITHELL]

ANONYMOUS (15th century)

Westphalian Song

When thou to my true-love com'st
Greet her from me kindly;
When she asks thee how I fare?
Say, folks in Heaven fare finely.

When she asks, "What! Is he sick?"
Say, dead!—and when for sorrow
She begins to sob and cry,
Say, I come tomorrow.

[SAMUEL TAYLOR COLERIDGE]

Anglo-Saxon and Middle English

Since most of the poems of considerable interest that might come into this group are not lyrics or, if so, are much too long to include, the selection here is rather in the nature of a token. However, much of the omitted material should be already familiar to the reader from courses in school. In spite of this assumption, I have hesitated to include many poems from the Middle English period because of the difficulty some people might have in dealing with strange spellings and glosses. These poems are best when "untranslated" and will repay the slight effort needed to understand them. In order to facilitate the reading, I have made small changes in some words to bring them, where possible, closer to modern English. Because the greatest work of Chaucer, even with this sort of change and marginal gloss, would still be a formidable task, rather than a pleasure, for most readers, I have had to represent him not by a narrative poem from the great Canterbury Tales, *but by short poems which do not adequately reveal his stature and rich genius.*

The early English poetry, in Anglo-Saxon, is strongly Germanic in subject, language and feeling. It has the same conventions of diction—the

*uniform four-stress alliterative line and kennings as ornament. The
elegies printed below suggest the usual meditative mood of the shorter
poems, with the pervasive atmosphere of bleak seacoasts and moors,
and a civilized tone with courtly attitudes. Much religious poetry, some
of it by the only known writers of the time—Caedmon and Cynewulf—
was written in the next century.*

*After the Norman Conquest (1066), the language and consequently
the poetry began to change. Alliterative verse gave way before rhymed
accentual lines and stanzas, (just as quantitative meter did in Latin)
though it continued to be written in certain regions till the fourteenth
century. With the Normans came French culture and taste in letters,
at first only in the court. Social conditions were not yet ripe for the
flourishing of a great literature. There is a mass of lovely lyrics, songs
and carols from these years, and many longer impressive works. But
it is only in Chaucer that we reach the supreme height at the end of the
Middle Ages in England.*

ANONYMOUS (8th century?)

The Wife's Lament

A song I sing of sorrow unceasing,
The tale of my trouble, the weight of my woe,
Woe of the present, and woe of the past,
Woe never-ending of exile and grief,
But never since girlhood greater than now.
First, the pang when my lord departed,
Far from his people, beyond the sea;
Bitter the heartache at break of dawn,
The longing for rumor in what far land
So weary a time my loved one tarried.
Far I wandered then, friendless and homeless,
Seeking for help in my heavy need.

With secret plotting his kinsmen purposed
To wedge us apart, wide worlds between,
And bitter hate. I was sick at heart.
Harshly my lord bade lodge me here.
In all this land I had few to love me,
Few that were loyal, few that were friends.
Wherefore my spirit is heavy with sorrow
To learn my beloved, my dear man and mate
Bowed by ill-fortune and bitter in heart,
Is masking his purpose and planning a wrong.
With blithe hearts often of old we boasted
That nought should part us save death alone;
All that has failed and our former love
Is now as if it had never been!
Far or near where I fly there follows
The hate of him who was once so dear.
In this forest-grove they have fixed my abode
Under an oak in a cavern of earth,
An old cave-dwelling of ancient days,
Where my heart is crushed by the weight of my woe.
Gloomy its depths and the cliffs that o'erhang it,
Grim are its confines with thorns overgrown—
A joyless dwelling where daily the longing
For an absent loved one brings anguish of heart.
Lovers there are who may live their love,
Joyously keeping the couch of bliss,
While I in my earth-cave under the oak
Pace to and fro in the lonely dawn.
Here must I sit through the summer-long day,
Here must I weep in affliction and woe;
Yet never, indeed, shall my heart know rest
From all its anguish, and all its ache,
Wherewith life's burdens have brought me low.
Ever man's years are subject to sorrow,
His heart's thoughts bitter, though his bearing be blithe;
Troubled his spirit, beset with distress—
Whether all wealth of the world be his lot,

Or hunted by Fate in a far country
My beloved is sitting soul-weary and sad,
Swept by the storm, and stiff with the frost,
In a wretched cell under rocky cliffs
By severing waters encircled about—
Sharpest of sorrows my lover must suffer
Remembering always a happier home.
Woeful his fate whose doom is to wait
With longing heart for an absent love.

[CHARLES W. KENNEDY]

The Seafarer

May I for my own self song's truth reckon,
Journey's jargon, how I in harsh days
Hardship endured oft.
Bitter breast-cares have I abided,
Known on my keel many a care's hold,
And dire sea-surge, and there I oft spent
Narrow nightwatch nigh the ship's head
While she tossed close to cliffs. Coldly afflicted,
My feet were by frost benumbed.
Chill its chains are; chafing sighs
Hew my heart round and hunger begot
Mere-weary mood. Lest man know not
That he on dry land loveliest liveth,
List how I, care-wretched, on ice-cold sea,
Weathered the winter, wretched outcast
Deprived of my kinsmen;
Hung with hard ice-flakes, where hail-scur flew,
There I heard naught save the harsh sea
And ice-cold wave, at whiles the swan cries,

Did for my games the gannet's clamour,
Sea-fowls' loudness was for me laughter,
The mews' singing all my mead-drink.
Storms, on the stone-cliffs beaten, fell on the stern
In icy feathers; full oft the eagle screamed
With spray on his pinion.
                                        Not any protector
May make merry man faring needy.
This he little believes, who aye in winsome life
Abides 'mid burghers some heavy business,
Wealthy and wine-flushed, how I weary oft
Must bide above brine.
Neareth nightshade, snoweth from north,
Frost froze the land, hail fell on earth then,
Corn of the coldest. Nathless there knocketh now
The heart's thought that I on high streams
The salt-wavy tumult traverse alone.
Moaneth alway my mind's lust
That I fare forth, that I afar hence
Seek out a foreign fastness.
For this there's no mood-lofty man over earth's midst,
Not though he be given his good, but will have in his youth
                                                                    greed;
Nor his deed to the daring, nor his king to the faithful
But shall have his sorrow for sea-fare
Whatever his lord will.
He hath not heart for harping, nor in ring-having
Nor winsomeness to wife, nor world's delight
Nor any whit else save the wave's slash,
Yet longing comes upon him to fare forth on the water.
Bosque taketh blossom, cometh beauty of berries,
Fields to fairness, land fares brisker,
All this admonisheth man eager of mood,
The heart turns to travel so that he then thinks
On flood-ways to be far departing.
Cuckoo calleth with gloomy crying,
He singeth summerward, bodeth sorrow,

The bitter heart's blood. Burgher knows not—
He the prosperous man—what some perform
Where wandering them widest draweth.
So that but now my heart burst from my breastlock,
My mood 'mid the mere-flood,
Over the whale's acre, would wander wide.
On earth's shelter cometh oft to me,
Eager and ready, the crying lone-flyer,
Whets for the whale-path the heart irresistibly,
O'er tracks of ocean; seeing that anyhow
My lord deems to me this dead life
On loan and on land, I believe not
That any earth-weal eternal standeth
Save there be somewhat calamitous
That, ere a man's tide go, turn it to twain.
Disease or oldness or sword-hate
Beats out the breath from doom-gripped body.
And for this, every earl whatever, for those speaking after—
Laud of the living, boasteth some last word,
That he will work ere he pass onward,
Frame on the fair earth 'gainst foes his malice,
Daring ado, . . .
So that all men shall honour him after
And his laud beyond them remain 'mid the English,
Aye, for ever, a lasting life's-blast,
Delight 'mid the doughty.
                              Days little durable,
And all arrogance of earthen riches,
There come now no kings nor Caesars
Nor gold-giving lords like those gone.
Howe'er in mirth most magnified,
Whoe'er lived in life most lordliest,
Drear all this excellence, delights undurable!
Waneth the watch, but the world holdeth.
Tomb hideth trouble. The blade is layed low.
Earthly glory ageth and seareth.
No man at all going the earth's gait,

But age fares against him, his face paleth,
Grey-haired he groaneth, knows gone companions,
Lordly men, are to earth o'ergiven,
Nor may he then the flesh-cover, whose life ceaseth,
Nor eat the sweet nor feel the sorry,
Nor stir hand nor think in mid heart,
And though he strew the grave with gold,
His born brothers, their buried bodies
Be an unlikely treasure hoard.

[EZRA POUND]

ANONYMOUS (11th century)

The Grave

For you was a house built   before you were born,
Earth marked out   ere you came from your mother.
But it was not made ready,   nor the depth of it reckoned,
Nor yet was it measured   how long it must be.
Now men bring you   where you needs must lie;
Now men measure you,   and the mold thereafter.
This house of yours   is not timbered high,
But low and level,   when you lie therein.
Low are the sills,   and low the side-walls;
Close to your breast   the roof is built.
Full cold shall you lie   in that lodging of mold,
Dark and dim;   the den decays,
A house without doors,   and dark within.
Long you'll be locked there,   and death has the key.
Loathsome that earth-house   and hateful to live in;
There you shall bide   and be wasted by worms.

Thus are you laid,   leaving your dear ones,
And never a friend   will fare to see you,
Or ever look   how you like the house,
Or undo the door,   and descend to join you,
For soon you'll be loathsome   and hateful to see.
Soon shall your head   be despoiled of hair,
And all the fairness   of your locks be faded;
Soft fingers shall stroke it   never again.

[CHARLES W. KENNEDY]

ANONYMOUS (*c.* 1260)

Summer

Sumer is icumen in,
    Lhude sing cuccu;
Groweth seed and bloweth med
    And springeth the wude nu.
        Sing cuccu!

Ewe

Loweth . . . cow;

*frisks . . . runs to the
        wood,*

Awe bleteth after lomb,
    Lhouth after calve cu;
Bulluc sterteth, bucke verteth,
    Murie sing cuccu.

cease thou never

Cuccu, cuccu, wel singes thu, cuccu:
    Na swike thu naver nu;
Sing cuccu, nu, sing cuccu,
    Sing cuccu, sing cuccu, nu.

ROBERT MANNYNG OF BRUNNE (1288–1338)

Woman's Love

No thyng is to man so dere
As wommanys love in gode manere.
A gode womman is mannys blys,
There her love right and stedfast is.
There is no solas under heavene,
Of alle that a man may nevene,   *name*
That shuld a man do so moche glew   *gladness*
As a gode womman that loveth trew.
Ne derer is none in Goddys hurde   *flock*
Than a chaste womman with lovely worde.

ANONYMOUS (14th–15th centuries)

Spring Song

Lenten is come with love to towne,
With blossem and with briddes roune,   *birds' cries,*
   That al this blisse bringeth.
Dayes-eyes in this dales,
Notes swete of nightegales,
   Uch fowl song singeth.
The threstlecok him threteth oo,   *ever chides,*
Away is huere winter wo,   *their*
   When woderove springeth.   *woodruff*
This fowles singeth ferly fele,   *wondrous many,*
And wlyteth on huere winne wele,   *warble in their wealth*
   That al the wode ringeth.   *of joy,*

clothes herself in red,

sends out her glow,

lovesome to see,

thyme.

Woo these

make merry their mates,

that flows

Lovers moan, . . .
          more:
I know I . . . those

The rose rayleth hire rode,
The leves on the lighte wode
    Waxen al with wille.
The moone mandeth hire bleo,
The lilye is lossom to seo,
    The fenil and the fille.
Wowes this wilde drakes:
Males murgeth huere makes,
    On streme that striketh stille.
Mody meneth, so doth mo:
Ichot ich am one of tho
    For love that likes ille.

Lustily.

make dank

Animals . . . secret
         cries,
Whereby to converse;

woo under clod;

The moone mandeth hire light;
So doth the seemly sonne bright,
    When briddes singeth breme.
Dewes donketh the downes;
Deores whisperes dernes rounes,
    Domes for to deme;
Wormes woweth under cloude;
Wimmen waxeth wounder proude,
    So wel hit wol them seme.

want for joy in one,

wealth of joy I

be fugitive.

Yf me shal wonte wille of on,
This wunne wele I wol forgon,
    And wight in wode be fleme.

Song of Ploughing

The merthe of alle this londe
Maketh the gode husbonde,
With erynge of his plowe.   *ploughing of*
I-blessed be Christes sonde,   *message,*
That hath us sent in honde
Merthe & joye y-nowe.

The plowe goth mony a gate,   *way,*
Bothe erly & eke late,
In wynter in the clay,
A-boute barly and whete,
That maketh men to swete;
God spede the plowe al day.

Browne Morel & Gore
Drawen the plowe ful sore
Al in the morwenynge;   *morning;*
Rewarde them, ther-fore
With a shefe or more
Alle in the evenynge.

Whan men be-gynne to sowe
Ful wel here corne they knowe
In the mounthe of May.
Howe ever Janyuer blowe,
Whether hye or lowe,
God spede the plowe all-way.

Whan men by-gynneth to wede
The thistle fro the sede
In somer, when they may,
Gode lete them wel to spede
& longe gode lyfe to lede,
All that for plowe-men pray.

Adam Lay Bound

Adam lay i-bowndyn,
  bowndyn in a bond,
Fowre thowsand wynter
  thowt he not to long;
And al was for an appil,
  an appil that he tok,
As clerkes fyndyn wretyn
  in here book.
Ne haddé the appil také ben
  the appil taken ben,
Ne haddé never our lady
  a ben hevené qwen.
Blyssid be the tyme
  that appil také was,
Therefore we mown syngyn
  Deo gracias.

scholars find written
in their

may sing

The Lytyll Prety Nyghtyngale

The lytyll prety nyghtyngale
Among the leavys grene,
I wold I were wyth her all nyght.
But yet ye wot not whome I mene.

The nyghtyngale sat on a brere
Among the thornys sherpe and keyn,
And comfort me wyth mery cher.
But yet ye wot not whome I mene.

She dyd apear all on hur kynde   *by nature*
A lady ryght well besene;
With wordys of loff tolde me hur mynde.
But yet ye wot not whome I mene.

Hyt dyd me goode upon hur to loke;
Her corse was closyd all in grene;   *clothed all*
Away fro me hur hert she toke.
But yet ye wot not whome I mene.

"Lady," I cryed wyth rufull mone,
"Have mynd of me that true hath bene;
For I love none but you alone."
But yet ye wot not whome I mene.

GEOFFREY CHAUCER (*c.* 1340–1400)

Ballade

thy golden
Hyde, Absalon, thy gilte tresses clere;
Esther, lay thou thy meeknesse al a-doun;
Hyde, Jonathas, al thy friendly mannere;
Penalopee, and Marcia Catoun,—
Mak of your wyfhood no comparisoun;
Hyde ye your beauties, Isoude and Eleyne;
may bedim.
My lady cometh, that al this may disteyne.

Thy faire body, let hit not appere,
Lavyne; and thou, Lucresse of Rome toun,
And Polixene, that boughten love so dere,
And Cleopatre, with al thy passioun,
Hyde ye your trouthe of love and your renoun;
And thou, Tisbe, that hast of love swich peyne;
My lady cometh, that al this may disteyne.

all together,
Hero, Dido, Laudomia, alle y-fere,
And Phyllis, hanging for thy Demophoun,
And Canace, espyed by thy chere,
Ysiphile, betraysed with Jasoun,
Maketh of your trouthe neyther boost ne soun;
Nor Ypermistre or Adriane, ye tweyne;
My lady cometh, that al this may disteyne.

Rondel

Now welcome, somer, with thy sunne softe,
That hast this wintres wedres overshake,   *weather shaken off,*
And driven away the longe nyghtes blake!   *black*

Saynt Valentyn, that art ful hy on-lofte,   *high aloft*
Thus syngen smale foules for thy sake:
Now welcome, somer, with thy sunne softe,
That hast this wintres wedres overshake.

Wel han they cause for to gladen ofte,   *be glad often*
Sith ech of them recovered hath hys make,   *mate*
Ful blissful mowe they synge when they wake:
Now welcome, somer, with thy sunne softe,
That hast this wintres wedres overshake,
And driven away the longe nyghtes blake!

The Complaint Unto Pity

so long ago,   Pitee, that I have sought so yore agoo,

anxious pain,   With herte soore, and ful of besy peyne,

so woeful   That in this world was never wight so woo

feign,   Withoute deth,—and, yf I shal not feyne,

My purpos was to Pitee to compleyne

Upon the crueltee and tirannye

Of Love, that for my trouthe doth me dye.

And when that I, bi lengthe of certeyne yeres,

Had continually   Had evere in oon a tyme sought to speke,

sprinkled with   To Pitee ran I, al bespreynt with teres,

me to avenge.   To prayen hir on Crueltee me awreke.

But er I myght with any word outbreke,

smart,   Or tellen any of my peyne's smerte,

I fond hir ded, and buried in an herte.

Adoun I fel when that I saugh the herse,

the swoon   Ded as a ston, while that the swogh me laste;

But up I roos, with colour ful dyverse,

And pitously on hir myn eyen I caste,

closely,   And ner the corps I gan to pressen faste,

I prepared   And for the soule I shop me for to preye.

I nas but lorn; ther was no more to seye.

Thus am I slayn, sith that Pitee is ded.

Allas, that day! that ever hyt shulde falle!

What maner man dar now hold up his hed?

To whom shal any sorwful herte calle?

device to slay   Now Crueltee hath cast to slee us alle,

without counsel of   In ydel hope, folk redeless of peyne,—

Syth she is ded, to whom shul we compleyne?

But yet encreseth me this wonder newe,
That no wight woot that she is ded, but I—   *no man knows*
So many men as in her tyme hir knewe—
And yet she dyed not so sodeynly;
For I have sought hir ever ful besely   *busily*
Sith first I hadde wit or mannes munde;
But she was ded er that I konde hir fynde.

Aboute hir herse there stoden lustely,   *stood happily*
Withouten any woe, as thoughte me,
Bountee[1] parfyt, wel armed and richely,
And fresshe Beautee, Lust, and Jolytee,
Assured Maner, Youthe, and Honestee,
Wisdom, Estaat, Drede, and Governaunce,
Confedred both by bond and alliaunce.

A compleynt had I, written, in myn hond,
For to have put to Pittee as a bille;
But when I al this companye ther fond,
That rather wolden al my cause spille
Than do me help, I held my pleynte stille;
For to that folk, withouten any fayle,
Withoute Pitee ther may no bille availe.

Then leve I al these vertues, sauf Pitee,   *except Pity*
Kepynge the corps, as ye have herd me seyn,   *me say,*
Confedered alle by bond of Crueltee,
And ben assented when I shal be sleyn.
And I have put my complaynt up ageyn;
For to my foes my bille I dar not shew,
Th'effect of which saith thus, in wordes fewe:—

[1] Bountee—Goodness; Lust—Pleasure; Jolytee—merriment; Maner—Courtesy; Honestee—Honor; Estaat—Rank; Drede—Dread; Governaunce—Demeanor.

The Bill of Complaint

Humblest of herte, highest of reverence,
Benygne flower, coroune of vertues alle,
your regal   Sheweth unto youre rial excellence
Youre servaunt, yf I durste me so calle,
mortal grief   Hys mortal harm, in which he is yfalle;
ill conduct,   And noght al oonly for his evel fare,
But for your renoun, as he shal declare.

your opponent   Hit stondeth thus: your contraire, Crueltee,
your authority   Allyed is ayenst your regalye,
Under the colour of womanly Beautee,—
For men shulde not, lo, knowe hir tirannye,—
With Bountee, Gentilesse, and Curtesye,
And hath depryved yow now of your place
is called . . .   That hyghte "Beautee apertenant to Grace."
appertaining to

For kyndely, by youre herytage ryght,
Ye ben annexed ever unto Bountee;
And verrayly ye oughte do youre myght
To helpe Trouthe in his adversytee.
Ye be also the corowne of Beautee;
lack these two,   And certes, yf ye wanten in these twayne,
is lost;   The world is lore; ther is no more to sayne.

and Nobility   Eke what availeth Maner and Gentilesse
Withoute yow, benygne creature?
Shal Crueltee be your governeresse?
Allas! what herte may hyt longe endure?
take care   Wherfore, but ye the rather take cure
To breke that perilouse alliaunce,
Ye sleen hem that ben in your obeisaunce.

And further over, yf ye suffre this,
Youre renoun ys fordoo than in a throwe; *killed then in a short time*
Ther shal no man wite wel what Pitee is. *know well*
Allas, that your renoun sholde be so lowe!
Ye be than fro youre heritage ythrowe *thrown out*
By Crueltee, that occupieth youre place;
And we despeyred, that seken to your grace. *are full of despair, that seek*

Have mercy on me, thow Herenus quene, *queen of Furies*
That yow have sought so tendirly and yore;
Let som strem of youre lyght on me be sene
That love and drede yow, ever lenger the more.
For, sothly for to seyne, I bere the soore;
And, though I be not cunnynge for to pleyne,
For Goddis love, have mercy on my peyne!

My peyne is this, that what I so desire
That have I not, ne nothing lyk therto;
And ever setteth Desir myn hert on fire.
Eke on that other syde, where so I goo,
What maner thing that may encrese my woo, *woe,*
That have I redy, unsoght, everywhere;
Me ne lakketh but my deth, and than my bere. *bier.*

What nedeth to shew parcel of my peyne?
Syth every woe that herte may bethynke
I suffre, and yet I dar not to yow pleyne;
For wel I wot, although I wake or wynke, *sleep,*
Ye rekke not whether I flete or synke. *You care . . . float*
But natherless, yet my trouthe I shal sustene
Unto my deth, and that shal wel be sene.

say,   This is to seyne, I wol be youres evere;
                    Though ye me slee by Crueltee, your foe,
Wholly my   Algate my spirit shal never dissevere
                    Fro youre servise, for any peyne or woe.
                    Sith ye be ded—allas, that hyt is so!—
                    Thus for your deth I may wel wepe and pleyne
                    With herte sore, and ful of besy peyne.

ANONYMOUS (15th century)

Song

Western wind, when will thou blow
The small rain down can rain?
Christ, if my love were in my arms
And I in my bed again!